F I N E
WATERS

FINE
WATERS

A CONNOISSEUR'S GUIDE
TO THE WORLD'S MOST DISTINCTIVE
BOTTLED WATERS

BY MICHAEL MASCHA

QUIRK BOOKS
PHILADELPHIA

FineWaters, FineWaters Balance, Virginality, Orientation, and Minerality are
trademarks of FineWaters Media, LLC. All rights reserved.

Library of Congress Cataloging in Publication Number: 2006928219

ISBN-10: 1-59474-119-0
ISBN-13: 978-1-59474-119-7

Printed in China

Typeset in Sabon and Gill Sans

Designed by Doogie Horner
Production management by Stephanie O'Neill McKenna

Photos on pages 12–13, 66–67, 75, 78, 79, 84, 85, 92, 94, 99, 100, 103, 104, 106,
110, 113, 115, 118, 120, 121, 126, 127, 134, 140, 141, 143, 145, 149, 153, 159,
160, and 172–173 by Steve Legato
Photos on pages 88 and 170 by Robert Marksteiner
All other images of bottles kindly provided by bottlers and distributors.

Distributed in North America by Chronicle Books
85 Second Street
San Francisco, CA 94105

10 9 8 7 6 5 4 3 2 1

Quirk Books
215 Church Street
Philadelphia, PA 19106
www.quirkbooks.com

CONTENTS

INTRODUCTION

"My books are water; those of the great geniuses are wine.
Everybody drinks water."
    —MARK TWAIN (1835–1910)

In the spring of 2002, my cardiologist gave me a choice: I could
either continue to drink wine or continue to live. Since I had
about five hundred bottles of wine stored in my wine cellar, I
hesitated.

Food and wine have always been an important part of my life.
For many years, as an academic food anthropologist, my interest in
food and wine was local and usually inexpensive—I was interested
in food as a distinct expression of a particular people and region.

When my wife's parents, who lived in a small Austrian village
ten miles (16 km) from the Iron Curtain, killed a pig, they used every
part of the animal. Preserved correctly by smoking, curing, and other
means, it would provide food for about six months. I'll spare you the
details of the dishes they made, but I will say it was some of the best
food I ever ate. It was also some of the most honest, and it really got
me interested in cooking.

In the later part of the eighties, my wife and I lived for about
three years on a very small and remote island in the Fiji archipelago.

Doing food-related research for my PhD, I encountered again the same dedication to food and the incredible knowledge of it developed by the people who had lived in that small ecosystem for about a hundred generations.

After thinking further about the choice my cardiologist had given me, I decided that eliminating wine from my life was probably the right choice. Pretty quickly I prepared my wine collection for long-term storage, in case I became terminally ill and could start drinking again.

I immediately noticed the void created by not being able to enjoy or even handle wine in an epicurean setting at home or in restaurants. I missed not just the taste, but the rituals surrounding wine—the swirling, the smelling, the pouring, the conversation. Though I never smoked, I know former smokers who tell me they miss the ritual and handling in a similar way.

It was time to look for alternatives. Instead of wine, I was now drinking water with meals. After the humiliation of toasting with a heavy water tumbler in a group of Riedel Sommeliers stemware and the frustration of the same old "still or sparkling" choice in restaurants that had award-winning wine lists, I decided something needed to change.

What was lacking, I realized, was attention to bottled water in an epicurean context and an overall etiquette for bottled water. Americans have recently started recognizing many food items, such as wine and olive oil, for their unique and cherished sources. Other items, like dark chocolate and salt, are currently undergoing that transition. But bottled water is still treated as a commodity lacking this *terroir*—the distinctive flavor determined by the local characteristics of the source. In many cases, bottled water is also held hostage to big brands with huge marketing powers.

But as with so many things, new worlds open up to those who look closely enough. By paying intelligent attention to what I was drinking, I discovered the world of fine bottled water. Water's total absence of smell and of visual variety makes one think all bottled waters are uniform, without any distinguishing characteristics. But as I started drinking different waters during a single meal, clear differences emerged. Suddenly terms like "focused and short," "broad and lingering," "substantial," or "light" seemed appropriate to describe the waters. With the help of the Internet, I was able to share my discoveries with the rest of the world.

And the world was ready. The FineWaters Web site (www.finewaters.com) quickly became a global destination for water connoisseurs by providing information on the bottled waters, creating an etiquette for them, and matching water with food.

This book is meant to provide you with the basics of bottled water connoisseurship and etiquette. Inside you'll learn about bottled water as a natural product with its own terroir. You'll also learn to distinguish fine bottled waters from commodity waters that also happen to be sold in bottles. You'll be able to select the appropriate bottled water to pair with your food and discover the principle of mouthfeel while exploring one hundred of the world's best bottled waters.

Water is life—enjoy it!

MICHAEL MASCHA
michael@finewaters.com

GLOSSARY

Aquifer: A geological formation that stores a large amount of water, which may come to the surface through a spring or a well. Most aquifers are made of sand, gravel, or permeable rock and are surrounded by clay or another impervious substance. More than one aquifer may exist at various depths in the same location, separated by impermeable layers.

Artesian: Artesian aquifers are surrounded by impermeable rock, which puts the water under pressure. When the aquifer is tapped, the pressure will force the water up the well without the use of a mechanical aid.

Carbonation, Artificial: Water has been carbonated artificially since the late eighteenth century. Current carbonation techniques involve pressurizing carbon dioxide before adding it to the water—pressure increases the amount of carbon dioxide that will dissolve. Opening a bottle of water at the table releases pressure, allowing the carbon dioxide to form bubbles that hadn't previously been visible.

Carbonation, Natural: Carbonation occurs when carbon dioxide is dissolved in water, creating the effervescence that characterizes sparkling water. Under certain conditions—volcanic activity, for example—water emerges from the ground naturally carbonated. Naturally carbonated waters are rare and have historically been highly sought after for their supposed curative properties.

FineWaters Balance: The FineWaters Balance provides a scale to define the differences between various bottled waters based on carbonation level and the associated mouthfeel. The scale is made up of levels of increasing carbonation: Still, Effervescent, Light, Classic, and Bold.

Hardness: A water's calcium and magnesium levels add together to determine the water's hardness. Hard tap water (containing high levels of calcium and magnesium) makes cleaning more difficult and causes scaling in boilers and teakettles. Water is softened by ion exchange and the addition of sodium.

Mouthfeel: Mouthfeel describes the tactile sensation brought on by a food—perhaps crunchy, chewy, or sticky. The carbonation level of sparkling water contributes significantly to its mouthfeel.

PET: PET stands for "polyethylene terephthalate," a plastic resin. A type of polyester, it's the plastic commonly used to package soft drinks and water and is labeled with the number 1 on bottles and containers.

pH Factor or Orientation: The pH (for "potential hydrogen") measures water's level of acidity or alkalinity. On this scale, 1.0 to 6.9 is acidic, 7.0 is neutral, and 7.1 to 14.0 is alkaline (also referred to as basic). Sour tastes (such as that of vinegar) come from acids, whereas alkaline substances tend to taste bitter and may seem to have a slippery feel. In the 5 to 9 range, the pH factor plays a very minor role in the overall perception of water.

Terroir: The concept of terroir ("soil" in French) refers to having a taste of the earth or soil, or the influence of local earth upon a product's flavor. Wine is the product most commonly described as having terroir: Each wine has a unique sense of place—a characteristic aroma and flavor that come from a particular vineyard's or region's grapes, which are themselves influenced by local soil and climate.

All water begins as two hydrogen molecules and one oxygen molecule—but the similarities between waters end there. Water is a universal solvent and dissolves just about anything it encounters. Because water, which originates under the earth, is in contact with minerals and trace elements in the geological strata, it gathers a unique composition of minerals along the way. This provides water with terroir—literally.

Total Dissolved Solids (TDS) or Minerality: The amount of minerals dissolved in water is indicated as total dissolved solids, usually measured in milligrams per liter (mg/l). Most waters fall in a TDS range of 50 to 2,000 mg/l.

Vintage: The age of water does not define its quality or taste, but paying attention to a water's age and enjoying the story of a water's background can significantly contribute to the overall epicurean experience.

Virginality: Virginality indicates how protected a water is from its surroundings. It is determined by the water's level of nitrate, an inorganic compound made up of one nitrogen atom and three oxygen atoms. Nitrate is easily carried through soil by water: Heavy rainfall or irrigation may cause the substance to leach into the ground below the root zone, and it may subsequently find its way into groundwater. In its natural state, water has less than 1 mg/l of nitrate; higher levels typically reveal a compromised water.

| PART I |

THE STORY
OF WATER

A BRIEF HISTORY
OF BOTTLED WATER

Ours is the blue planet, and the hallmark of life on Earth is water. But where did this colorless, odorless liquid first come from?

Recent discoveries in astrophysics suggest that water is not native to Earth but rather was imported from the edges of our solar system as ice trapped in comets. Scientists think this water was first delivered here more than four billion years ago. During the meteor shower that gave the Moon most of its craters, Earth received five hundred times more "hits" than its moon did; since the planet has a greater critical mass than its satellite, Earth was also able to hold on to much of the water from the ice. The ice within comets traps noble gases as well as a cocktail of other chemicals, such as silicates, carbons, and interplanetary dust, so these elements have likely always been present in Earth's water. (Comets may have also brought amino acids, the building blocks of biogenetic activity, to Earth.)

Eventually, water became one of the most important substances on Earth—but for civilizations to advance, it needed to be controlled. This process began about ten thousand years ago with the development of agriculture, which required capturing, storing, and distributing water.

Ample, clean water is needed to sustain human culture, as the earliest, most successful civilizations recognized—after all, humans can live a month without food but only a week without water.

In ancient times, the Egyptians devised a number of filtration systems to make use of the Nile's silty waters. On the wall of Amenopthis II's tomb at Thebes (dated 1450 BCE), Nile water is depicted being siphoned through and clarified by a series of clay pots.

The Roman Empire built an extensive aqueduct system, an ambitious feat of engineering not surpassed until the twentieth century. At Rome's peak, eleven aqueducts served the city. The Romans were discriminating about water quality and judged each source

> Roman baths near thermal springs were built by battle-weary legionnaires as places to rest and heal. The baths provided them with *sanus per aquam*, or "health through water." The initials of that Latin phrase give us the modern word *spa*.

by the transparency and taste of its water. Aqua Marcia, which drew water from the Anio River 57 miles (92 km) away, was regarded as the aqueduct with the finest water. Pliny the Elder claimed its water was also the coldest. The next best water came from a spring 14 miles (23 km) to the north, carried by the Aqua Viro, which today ends at the Trevi Fountain. Other aqueducts, such as the Aqua Anio Novus and Aqua Anio Vetus (Tivoli), also fed off the Anio River but were regarded as slightly muddy.

Because water is necessary to life, it has spiritual meaning in every culture. In desert-based religions, for example, water is often a symbol of life or purification. Streams, springs, and spas have a long tradition of religious significance and have been especially associated with fertility. Many of the late–Bronze Age stone circles of the British Isles, for example, are associated with nearby wells. The shaft of one of these wells near Stonehenge is 100 feet (30.5 m) deep—impressive given the technology of the period. Beads and other small objects found nearby suggest that offerings were made to spirits. Archaeologists believe similar offerings have been made at the Sorgenti di Vicarello spring near Rome since the Stone Age, about ten thousand years ago. Who knew throwing pennies into a fountain in your local shopping mall belongs to a tradition thousands of years old?

Because water supplies were so polluted, hydration in medieval Europe was mainly accomplished with beer. Water diluted the beer to about one percent alcohol content—enough to minimize the effects of fecal bacteria in the water but not enough to intoxicate the drinker very much.

The health benefits of water sources formed a less superstitious basis for appreciation as Western civilization moved away from belief in gods and goddesses. Some sources revered by pagans, such as Lourdes, became places of pilgrimage for health purposes and retained some sense of mysticism.

With personal hygiene becoming a concern in late eighteenth-century Europe, visits to mineral springs, to drink or bathe in the curative waters, became fashionable. The trend was set by the wealthy, who could afford to "take the waters."

Some of these destinations gained fame as "water hospitals," among them Contrex in France and Fiuggi in Italy. Since the early eighteenth century, water from both these springs was thought to be beneficial to kidney stones. By the nineteenth century, numerous spa resorts were attracting the infirm and the idle vacationer. Many of these resorts and springs live on today as familiar European brand names: Evian, San Pellegrino, Perrier, Vittel, Vöslauer, Spa, Borsec, Chaudfontaine, Harrogate, and many more.

Many well-known curative waters have been distributed throughout Europe as luxury drinks since ancient Roman times. At first, the waters were typically free; the only cost was shipping. But the owners of the now-famous spas discovered they could earn revenue by selling the water for off-site use. This mineral water was sold in stoneware jars, porcelain demi-jars, and, later, glass containers and bottles.

Water emerges with the added bonus of natural carbonation from many famous sources (Vichy Catalan, Ferrarelle, Wattwiller, Apollinaris, and Perrier, for example). Artificial carbonation became possible in the late seventeenth century. The southwest German town of Niederselters, source of a naturally carbonated curative water, is the namesake for "Selters Water," or seltzer, as it became known.

Many waters still on the market today have fascinating histories. The reviews in Part II of this book detail each water's individual story further, but some waters are worth examining here for what they say about the bottled water industry as a whole.

Commercial exploitation of water sources began in France. Evian first opened a thermal bath on the private estate of the king of Sardinia in 1824. The king authorized sales of the water two years later, and a company was formed in 1829 to sell the water. It was first bottled in earthenware; Evian did not begin bottling in glass until 1920.

While marching to Rome in 218 BCE, Hannibal used the Perrier spring in the south of France. Use of the spring remained free until 1863, when Napoleon III sold the rights to it. The spring's namesake, Dr. Louis Perrier, and a local farmer bought the spa site in Vergèze in 1888 (Dr. Perrier gained full control of the site ten years later). Marketing the spring's naturally carbonated water was the brainchild of St. John Harmsworth, who purchased the spring from Dr. Perrier after recuperating at the spa in 1903. Harmsworth named the spring after Perrier to lend it a sense of medical authority; the iconic green bottle was designed to reflect the Indian clubs or weighted skittles Harmsworth used for sport while convalescing.

Other European countries soon followed the French in selling their waters. England introduced what's thought to be its first bottled water, Malvern, at the Great Exhibition of 1851 in London. Germany's Apollinaris received a red triangle award—an indication of outstanding quality—at a British trade show in 1892 and later registered the symbol as its trademark. San Pellegrino packed 35,343 bottles during 1899, the Italian water's first year of sales; by 1908 it was being exported throughout the world, even to remote places like Peru, China, and Australia.

In North America, meanwhile, Native Americans had been bathing together in thermal mineral springs for physical, spiritual, and social health since long before the arrival of European settlers. Many of the waters were thought to have healing powers.

> Polluted and unsanitary municipal water supplies during the seventeeth through nineteenth centuries meant that spas offered curative benefits by default: The spring water might not have been magically healthful, but it was an improvement over the contaminated city water.

Water from Jackson's Spa in Boston was bottled as early as 1767 and sold as a curative. Mineral water from near Albany, New York, was bottled commercially around 1800, and twenty years later Saratoga Springs sold its first bottled water. Mountain Valley Spring began bottling in 1871.

The bottling of natural mineral waters reached its height in the late nineteenth century; the rising popularity of "soda waters" then began to elbow mineral water out of the market. The latter was at this time sold primarily as a curative and a luxury drink for the wealthy.

Clever marketing strategies were applied to reinvigorate the natural bottled water market. Evian again took the lead in the 1950s by selling its water with the powerful claim, "to help lactating mothers and [provide] important minerals for infants." Targeting a new generation of consumers showed great foresight, as this demographic turned out to be the baby boomers, who took Evian to the top of the bottled mineral water market.

BOTTLED WATER TODAY

T oday about three thousand brands of bottled water are available around the world. The growing trend has generated a large demand, and almost every day a new bottled water brand or company is born.

In the United States, where bottled water has a less-developed history, several factors are responsible. Most Americans have had access to safe drinking water since the early twentieth century, when municipal supplies began to be disinfected. Chlorination went a long way toward stopping waterborne diseases, and as the population replaced bottled water with tap water, the bottled water industry was devastated. But the public tends to view municipal water supplies negatively, and indeed some areas have suffered from poorer quality in recent decades. This has encouraged the bottled water trend, as have pushes for healthy living and successful marketing by water companies. Bottled water is in style, and its American sales have increased from about $50 million in 1960 to about $5 billion in 2000.

But all bottled water is not necessarily equal, as we will see.

All bottled waters, still or sparkling, can be categorized as either processed municipal water or natural bottled water. Most bottled water sold in Europe is natural bottled water, and it's most often consumed at home and in restaurants. Most Europeans prefer to sit at a table when drinking water rather than drinking it on the go. Italians drink more bottled water than any other nationality—189 liters (50 gallons) per capita each year, according to a 2005 study—but only six percent of it is consumed away from the table. In fact, Italians consider it rude to eat or drink when not seated at a table.

In contrast, thirty-five percent of Americans' bottled water is consumed on the go.

> Nestlé dominates the hospitality sector of the bottled water market—especially in the carbonated water category—with the omnipresent San Pellegrino. Unfortunately many restaurants still sell bottles of San Pellegrino for hugely marked-up prices.

Americans drank 69 liters (18 gallons) of bottled water per capita during the same study, and much of it was processed municipal water. Much credit for opening the U.S. market to bottled water goes to Perrier, which succeeded in positioning its water as a healthy-living staple in the late 1970s.

Paris-based Groupe Danone and the Swiss company Nestlé are the two main players in today's global bottled water market. Danone's main properties are Evian and Volvic; Nestlé sells other familiar names, such as Perrier, San Pellegrino, Vittel, Contrex, Panna, Deer Park, and Poland Spring. Also taking up shelf space in the U.S. market are Coca-Cola's Dasani and PepsiCo's Aquafina water, both processed from municipal sources. Small distributors can't offer supermarkets the price and volume advantages of the large companies, so high-end bottled waters often end up in smaller grocery or gourmet stores, limiting their availability.

To overcome some of these geographic and marketing limitations, water distributors have turned to the Internet to sell hard-to-source bottled waters. To be sure, the shipping charges usually double the price, but that hasn't deterred online shoppers. Consumers want natural bottled water.

As the trend toward natural bottled water has increased, consumers have become more educated and demand options beyond simply still or sparkling—much as a choice between only "red wine" and "white wine" would be considered inadequate in a restaurant. Water menus, much like wine lists, are now available in some establishments to point out bottled waters that affirm or contrast the options on the chef's food menu. Like wine, natural waters come from a unique source. And also like wine, water has terroir.

THE MYTH OF PURE WATER

Marketing campaigns for commodity bottled waters try to make us think water must be "pure" to be good. Being clean and healthy isn't enough—water has to be pure, and the purer the better. These marketers tell us that nothing but hydrogen and oxygen should be in our water. Ironically, this misconception means people often drink distilled water when taking mineral supplements, which contain the same minerals that have been removed from the water.

The advertising for commodity waters points to two of our water-drinking preferences: We like water cold, and we like it clear. Each of these inclinations is grounded in human evolution—bacteria has a harder time growing in cold water, and the presence of microorganisms can be indicated by cloudy water.

Even distillation, which removes more contaminants than any other purification method, does not produce completely "pure" water. Rising steam is supposed to leave all impurities behind in the distilling process, but in fact gases, some chemicals, and some organic compounds can be taken along with the steam. Active carbon filters are used to eliminate those remaining contaminants from distilled water, but some impurity remains with this process, too.

In reverse osmosis (RO), water molecules are forced

> Water's "impurities" can actually be beneficial: The carbonic acid that gives sparkling water its effervescence is a mild antiseptic.

through a rubber membrane, leaving impurities behind. But gases, some chemicals (including chloramine and arsenic), and some bacteria can beat this technique, too.

So there is no such thing as pure water. It's a myth. Natural water has mineral content. By removing minerals, water becomes acidic and "aggressive," meaning it will seek to replace the minerals removed. Water treated by either distillation or RO will become acidic upon contact with air—airborne carbon dioxide reacts with the water, taking the place of the removed minerals or contaminants.

Because water is a universal solvent, rainwater collects particles and chemicals even as it's falling. Geological strata only add more to the composition—the minerals and trace elements of the local area give each water its distinct terroir. Underground geology may filter water for decades or even millennia; when the water finally emerges at the source, it may not be "pure," but it is nevertheless clean and healthy.

Clean, healthy water does not have to be pure. In fact, the waters with the most epicurean interest contain minerals and trace elements.

THE DIFFERENCE BETWEEN *BOTTLED* WATER AND BOTTLED *WATER*

Much bottled water is really bottled municipal tap water—in the United States, government and industry estimate that municipal water makes up twenty-five to forty percent of the bottled water sold. American bottlers are also permitted by the FDA to label water as spring water even when it's treated with chemicals or pumped to the surface through a well near a true spring. For example, wells across southern Maine pump water to be sold as Nestlé's Poland Spring, which is sourced neither from Poland Spring nor any other spring.

It's helpful to make a distinction between two different kinds of bottled water.

BOTTLED WATER

The salient characteristic of this type is that it is bottled, providing a convenient package for on-the-go hydration. Water fountains or sinks would work just as well to quench your thirst, but water companies' self-serving marketing campaigns may have persuaded you that water is healthier when it comes from a bottle.

This attitude turns bottled water into a commodity, regardless of where the water comes from. Convenience is the key; the water itself is nothing special. The large, powerful companies behind these waters ensure that their products are the ones found in everyday supermarkets, unfortunately.

Water like this is the reason journalists sometimes condemn bottled water as a big scam, and I can understand their thinking. I would be angry, too, if I bought water in the supermarket only to discover that it was in fact purified tap water. But I'm not angry, because I know better: I buy bottled *water*.

BOTTLED *WATER*

These very special waters express terroir. Bottled at the source, they may be naturally carbonated and are treated only minimally (if at all). Contact with geological formations imparts a unique mineral composition to each water; many of these compositions are reputed to have healthful properties. Some waters may have been formed only thirty days before bottling, whereas others are more than twenty thousand years old.

Many companies and individuals care deeply about the water they sell and its source. I talk to them every day, and they could certainly talk about their product all day—they are proud of delivering natural bottled water and obsessed with protecting its source. Some of these companies are new, but sometimes the waters have been used since Roman times, more than two thousand years ago.

THE SOURCES OF WATER

R ain (and other precipitation) is the origin of all water. But after rainwater falls, geological and meteorological factors influence the next step in the journey. When winter snowfall in the Alps melts in springtime, it flows into rivers and the water table. Springs at the base of the mountain then bubble forth with this relatively young water. But in other parts of the world, the ground may quickly absorb falling rainwater, and the water may not reach the surface again for another ten thousand years. Much of what we drink today is rainwater that fell hundreds or thousands of years ago.

Water that circulates in a deep spring, well, or artesian well is generally more protected from human and animal waste than surface water or water from a shallow aquifer. But deep-circulating water often has a higher mineral content because it interacts with rocks for longer periods. Still, shallow-circulating water or even surface water may be of fine quality—environmental conditions make all the difference. From pristine and protected surroundings, shallow water and even rainwater are clean, safe, and delightful to drink.

Since the ultimate source of water is always rain, let's look a little more closely at the places where the water emerges or is extracted from the ground.

SPRING

More bottled waters claim springs as their origin than any other type of source. Spring waters vary widely in their mineral composition and TDS level, both of which are influenced by the geology of the local area. Some springs naturally carbonate the water. The best-tasting spring water comes from a protected, free-flowing spring and is treated as little as possible during the bottling process. Evian, Levissima, and Trinity are just a few examples of the many bottled spring waters.

The actual definition of spring water is controversial. Geologists characterize it as water flowing through the surface of the earth with no help from machines. But water from a borehole (a well) drilled next to the spring can also be considered spring water—by the U.S. Food and Drug Administration, at least—if a hydraulic link between the spring and the borehole can be shown, the water from both the borehole and the spring are chemically identical, the borehole does not prevent the spring's natural flow, and the borehole does not open the aquifer to surface water.

Using a spring's natural orifice, however, is preferable. When the water's own pressure brings it to the surface, that pressure can prevent contaminants in ground and surface water from mixing with the spring water. Boreholes may endanger a spring's life, too, as the volume of water extracted by a borehole is higher than the spring's natural capacity.

ARTESIAN

When an artesian aquifer is tapped, pressure in the aquifer will force the water up the well without the use of a mechanical aid. The aquifer is surrounded by impermeable rock and typically made of sandstone or other porous rocks or sediment. The pressure built up in a sloped aquifer will push water to the surface and may create a permanent fountain.

Artesian water matches spring water's range of characteristics. Vendors often promote a brand's "artesian" quality as a distinguishing factor. Examples of bottled artesian waters include Fiji and Voss.

WELL

Nonartesian wells need mechanical pumps to bring water from the aquifer to the surface.

Most people don't think highly of well water, so labels rarely trumpet such an origin. But this negative public opinion is unfair, as many blind water tastings favor well water over spring and artesian.

Well water is similar to spring water in its wide range of TDS and mineral composition. Highland Spring, Tau, and Hildon are examples of waters sourced from wells.

RAIN

Rainwater has historically been used to irrigate crops and supply drinking water; typically, it is harvested on rooftops and stored for later use. Many island nations use rainwater as a substantial part of their water supply. Even the roofs of skyscrapers in Hong Kong are used to collect rain.

Recently, companies began bottling rainwater falling in remote, unpolluted parts of the world. Several of these waters come from Tasmania, where air pollution is extremely negligible. Rainwater must be harvested carefully—to prevent contamination, the water must be stored quickly after it hits the collection surface.

Bottled rainwater is young water, with an extra-low mineral content. In most cases, it is nitrate free, though bottlers usually filter the water. Examples of bottled rainwaters include Cape Grim, Cloud Juice, and Oregon Rain.

GLACIER

About twenty thousand years ago, Earth was one-third covered by glaciers, the remains of which are now being tapped as a source for bottled water. Alaskan tidewater-calving glaciers are melted for bottling, and elsewhere the water is harvested just before it would run into the ocean. The sources' steep terrain is often inhospitable to humans or animals, and access is restricted by environmental regulations. Even so, some contamination concerns remain (see the discussion of icebergs below).

Glacier water is old water, sometimes formed more than seventeen thousand years ago. Typically, it has an extremely low mineral content and is similar in taste and other qualities to rainwater. Ice Age is one of the glacier waters that appear in this book.

ICEBERG

Twelve to fifteen thousand years ago, snow untouched by industrial pollution was compacted to form large glacial walls. These walls eventually became icebergs and were subjected to modern air pollution—thus, they may be contaminated, especially on the surface. Advertisers try to convince us of icebergs' unspoiled purity, but such claims are worth examination (especially in light of recent studies that found bacteria in glacial ice). Also keep in mind that icebergs contain a layer of ice formed in the 1950s, when air pollution was very high and atomic tests common—the results of which you're probably not dying to drink.

Today, icebergs are melted and bottled after they've been towed from the North Atlantic toward the Newfoundland shore and broken into pieces. Not surprisingly, Iceberg Water is an example of this type of bottled water.

LAKE, STREAM, OR RESERVOIR

Much municipal water is sourced from reservoirs, lakes, or streams and then highly purified (microfiltered and ozonated). In rare instances such water is also bottled and sold with a source designation—Hetch Hetchy Mountain Water, for example, comes from Hetch Hetchy Reservoir, San Francisco's main water source.

DEEP SEA

Icebergs near Greenland melted thousands of years ago, and the water produced was of a different temperature and salinity than the surrounding seawater. This difference kept the water separate as it sank to the ocean floor; it now circles Earth every several thousand years.

The Natural Energy Laboratory of Hawaii Authority (NELHA), at Keahole Point, Hawaii, provides access to this deep seawater through a pipeline reaching 3,000 feet (914 m) into the ocean. Entrepreneurs have begun bottling the desalinated water, mainly to be sold in the Japanese market. Kona Deep is an example of a bottled deep-sea water.

THE FLAVOR OF WATER

A t first glance, waters may not seem to have the individual characteristics that distinguish wines. But through comparison with the flavors in wine, subtle but distinct differences in water flavors become apparent, too. This chapter will examine the components of flavor as they apply to water.

FLAVOR = TASTE + SMELL + MOUTHFEEL

Taste, smell, and mouthfeel (a food's tactile sensation) combine to produce flavor. Sensory receptors in the nose and mouth report information on each of these three components to the brain, where the sensation is integrated in a highly complex process we are just beginning to understand.

Food writers often pay little attention to mouthfeel, but it is a very important property of both food and water. The size, amount, and distribution of bubbles—or lack of them—are essential to the mouthfeel of water. I use the FineWaters Balance to describe a water's mouthfeel (see page 43).

Here's a comparison of the elements of flavor in wine and water:

	TASTE	**SMELL**	**MOUTHFEEL**
WINE	complex	complex	uniform (with the exception of sparkling wine)
WATER	very subtle	absent	complex

Based on these factors, a wine tasting emphasizes taste and smell, whereas mouthfeel is the most important characteristic to consider in a water tasting.

TASTE

You may have seen a map of the tongue divided into regions sensitive to different tastes—salty, sweet, sour, bitter, and umami (savory). This misleading map originated in a mistranslated German thesis from the early twentieth century, which was disproven in 1974. Collections of cells called taste buds are spread across the tongue and the hard and soft palates; they are all sensitive to any kind of taste.

SMELL

We can perceive thousands of different odors, but unlike taste, no scheme to categorize basic smells has been established. Instead, the associated object usually lends its name to the smell: An orange may taste sweet, but it smells like an orange. Nerve cells that act as olfactory receptors have a lifespan of about thirty days. While chewing, we can perceive odors through both the nose and the oral cavity.

MOUTHFEEL AND TEXTURE

You may not be familiar with the term *mouthfeel*, but you know the concept if you can tell the difference in texture between a creamy pudding, a crunchy pickle, a crispy potato chip, and soft bread. Mouthfeel and texture have a lot of influence over how satisfying food is.

THE COMPOSITION OF WATER

Compared with wine, differences in taste among waters are quite subtle. But they are nevertheless discernible. Local geological strata impart water with different minerals, giving every single-source water a unique set of characteristics. This section describes the most common minerals found in bottled water as well as the benefits these minerals can provide.

MAGNESIUM (Mg^{++})

Almost all human cells contain some level of magnesium, and adults need three to four hundred milligrams of magnesium every day. Magnesium is important for the regulation of muscle contractions and the transmission of nerve impulses, and it activates energy-producing enzymes. Bone structure also relies on magnesium, and the element expands blood vessels, which lessens the risk of heart attack. Nervousness, lack of concentration, dizziness, and headaches or migraines may result from magnesium deficiency.

Most bottled waters have below 20 mg/l of magnesium, though Donat Mg is an extremely high example with 1,000 mg/l.

CALCIUM (Ca^{++})

Adults need about eight hundred milligrams of calcium per day; babies don't require as much, but fifteen- to nineteen-year-olds need significantly more. The many benefits of calcium include stabilizing bone structure, teeth, and cell membranes; ensuring nerve and muscle impulses are properly transmitted; and helping prevent blood clots. Bones decalcify (osteoporosis) and fractures become more likely if a body is not getting enough calcium.

Bottled water usually has less than 100 mg/l of calcium, but a few examples (such as Contrex and Sanfaustino) have about 500 mg/l.

POTASSIUM (K$^+$)

Two to four grams are usually a sufficient day's supply of potassium. Children and young people should pay particular attention to their intake, since potassium aids the growth of cells. The pressure of water between cells is regulated by potassium, which also makes sure each cell gets enough food. Potassium has special roles to play in muscle contraction and heartbeat. Potassium deficiency can weaken skeletal muscles and make smooth muscles tired.

Typical potassium content in bottled water is less than 5 mg/l, but some (such as Ferrarelle and Malavella) can have as much as 50 mg/l.

SODIUM (Na$^+$)

A person's level of exertion largely determines his or her daily requirement of sodium. Normally about three grams are necessary, but severe physical stress can bring the requirement up to fifteen grams or more. The heart's metabolism is affected by sodium, as is the regular contraction of the heart. Today, we rarely have to worry about sodium deficiency: Salt is an integral part of many foods, especially those that are highly processed.

Sodium ranges from 10 mg/l in most bottled waters to 1,200 mg/l in a few, such as Vichy Catalan and Vichy Célestins.

SULFATES (SO$_4^{2-}$)

Sulfates are the salts of sulfur. They help the liver detoxify the body and aid digestion by stimulating the gall bladder. Sulfates in high doses act as a laxative. Fish, meat, and milk contain sulfates, which are an important component of protein. The human body absorbs only small amounts of sulfates, but these amounts are sufficient to stimulate peristalsis by binding magnesium and sodium to water in the intestine. This effect makes mineral waters rich in sulfates, which taste slightly bitter, suitable as "nonalcoholic bitters" after a meal.

Most bottled waters have well below 100 mg/l of sulfates, but

San Pellegrino and a few others can reach 500 mg/l.

BICARBONATE (HCO$_3^-$)

Present in all biological fluids, bicarbonate is essential for maintaining our bodies' pH balance. The substance is also found in stomach secretions. Lactic acid generated by physical activity is neutralized by bicarbonate dissolved in water; a similar process raises the pH of some acidic foods.

The typical range for bicarbonate in bottled water is 50 to 200 mg/l, but it can reach up to about 1,800 mg/l in waters such as Apollinaris, Gerolsteiner, and Borsec.

SILICA (SiO$_2$)

Most adults need between twenty and thirty milligrams of silica daily. Silica reduces the risk of heart disease and may prevent osteoporosis; it also helps repair tissue by serving as an antioxidant. Hair and nails are strengthened by silica.

If bottled waters contain any silica, it's usually less than 20 mg/l; the higher levels in waters such as Fiji and Antipodes are well below 100 mg/l.

TRACE ELEMENTS

The human body needs iron, iodine, copper, fluoride, zinc, and other trace elements as well as minerals. The recommended daily intake is fractions of a milligram for some substances and a few milligrams for others.

TOTAL DISSOLVED SOLIDS (TDS)

Water's subtle taste and terroir are determined by the minerals it contains. The amount of minerals dissolved in water is indicated as total dissolved solids, measured in milligrams per liter (mg/l) or parts per million (ppm), which are equal. A water's TDS is normally made up mainly of carbonates, bicarbonates, chlorides, sulfates, phosphates, nitrates, calcium, magnesium, sodium, potassium, iron, manganese, and a few other minerals. Gases, colloids, or sediment is not included in the TDS measurement.

SUPER LOW	0–50 mg/l total dissolved solids
LOW	50–250 mg/l
MEDIUM	250–800 mg/l
HIGH	800–1,500 mg/l
VERY HIGH	>1,500 mg/l

After mouthfeel, TDS is the second most important factor in matching water with food. The higher the mineral content, the more distinct a water's taste can be. Think of low TDS waters as comparable to white wines, with a clean, neutral taste and less weight; high TDS waters are more like red wines, with a heavier, more substantial feel. Very high TDS waters feel distinctly heavy and may have an aftertaste, much like a big, bold red wine. Most mineral water you drink, though, probably has a medium TDS measurement and is more like a heavy white or a light red wine.

Regulations regarding TDS vary throughout the world. In the United States, bottled water must contain at least 250 mg/l TDS to be labeled as mineral water. TDS above 500 mg/l qualifies a water as "low mineral content"; more than 1,500 mg/l allows a "high mineral content" label.

Distilled water has a TDS of 0 mg/l; seawater has about 34,000 mg/l. Most bottled waters fall within a TDS range of 50 to 800 mg/l (Ducale, 55 mg/l; Panna, 188 mg/l; Fiji, 210 mg/l; Evian, 357 mg/l; Perrier, 475 mg/l), but many highly regarded waters have a much higher TDS (San Pellegrino, 1,109 mg/l; Badoit, 1,200 mg/l; Contrex, 2,032 mg/l; Gerolsteiner, 2,527 mg/l). Some of these waters are thought to be curatives—their mineral compositions are believed to have healing properties (Famous Crazy, 2,783 mg/l; Vichy Célestins, 3,378 mg/l). But some curative waters have a low TDS: Fiuggi, for example, has a TDS of only 122 mg/l.

ANALYZING WATER

The International Bottled Water Association (IBWA) requires bottlers to have an independent analysis conducted on their waters; bottlers usually make the information available on their Web sites. Founded in 1958, the IBWA is the bottled water industry's trade association and represents bottlers, distributors, and suppliers from around the world. It helps various levels of government regulate the industry to provide the best water possible.

The independent water analysis, known as Appendix A, lists each organic and inorganic chemical present in the water. Labels on bottled waters typically mention minerals found in the water, some of which may be noted as distinguishing factors. Other times, the absence of a particular mineral is pointed out in the same way.

HARDNESS

Calcium and magnesium levels combine to determine the water's "hardness" (for the exact formula, see the table below). Bottled water is naturally soft, thanks to low levels of calcium and magnesium. Higher levels are often found in municipal water, which is often "softened"—particularly in the United States—to be used at home. The taste of water is impacted heavily by softening. Hard tap water makes cleaning more difficult and more dependent on soaps and synthetic detergents. Scaling in boilers and teakettles comes from hard water. But hard water does not pose any danger to your health: According to the U.S. National Research Council, the magnesium and calcium in hard water can actually contribute to your daily dietary requirements.

Water is softened with an ion-exchange water softener, which adds sodium (salt) to the water. About 8 mg/l of sodium are added for every grain of hardness (17.1 mg/l) taken out. Water softening accustoms most Americans to slightly salty water.

In the United States, water hardness is not regulated by the Environmental Protection Agency. Instead the Department of the Interior and the international Water Quality Association offer the following classifications:

SOFT	0–17.1 mg/l	0–1.0 grains per gallon
SLIGHTLY HARD	17.1–60	1.0–3.5
MODERATELY HARD	60–120	3.5–7.0
HARD	120–180	7.0–10.5
VERY HARD	>180	>10.5

Hardness can be calculated with this formula (calcium and magnesium should be measured in milligrams per liter):

HARDNESS = (calcium x 2.5) + (magnesium x 4)

pH FACTOR

The pH (for "potential hydrogen") measures a substance's level of acidity or alkalinity. On this scale, 1.0 to 6.9 is acidic, 7.0 is neutral, and 7.1 to 14.0 is alkaline (also referred to as basic). Sour tastes (such as that of vinegar) come from acids, whereas alkaline substances tend to taste bitter and may seem to have a slippery feel. Low alkaline waters (pH 7.1–7.5) may be perceived as sweet—this doesn't mean that the water tastes sugary but simply that it tastes neither bitter nor sour.

Since pH is a logarithmic scale, the difference of 1 degree indicates a tenfold increase or decrease in acidity or alkalinity. Water with a pH of 5, for example is ten times more acidic than that with a pH of 6.

I find that my palate tends to register acidity as a major component of taste at a pH of 5 or below. The following is how I describe Orientation, or the taste of water based on the pH factor, as you'll see in my tasting notes:

pH OF COMMON SUBSTANCES

Vinegar	3
Wine	2.8–3.8
Beer	4–5
Milk	6.3–6.6
Seawater	8.3
Bottled water	5–10

ACIDIC	pH 5–6.7
NEUTRAL	pH 6.7–7.3
HINT OF SWEET	pH 7.3–7.8
ALKALINE	pH 7.8–10

Be sure not to let the pH factor have too much influence when considering the flavor of water. In the 5 to 10 range, the pH factor plays a minor role (contributing five percent of the flavor) relative to the TDS (twenty percent) and the carbonation (seventy-five percent).

CARBONATION

Because it adds mouthfeel, carbonation is the most important characteristic to consider when matching bottled water with food. Water is carbonated by dissolving carbon dioxide in it, which adds effervescence by creating a dilute carbonic acid solution. Carbonated water is also known as sparkling water, soda, or seltzer. The FineWaters Balance categorizes sparkling water by mouthfeel using five levels of carbonation (see page 43).

In a study published in 2001 by the *Journal of Medicinal Food*, high mineral content was found to be favorable for carbonated waters (within a specified limit) but not still waters. The report did find, however, that still waters with high mineral content made good mouth cleaners when drinking red wine.

NATURAL CARBONATION

Certain rare geological conditions can produce naturally carbonated water; often the carbonation can be attributed to volcanic activity. Naturally carbonated waters have historically been highly sought after for their supposed curative properties. The carbon dioxide helps this water absorb minerals in high levels.

Apollinaris is an example of a naturally carbonated water. Volcanic activity in the Eifel region of Germany enriches the water there with minerals, and magma gives off carbon dioxide. Other naturally carbonated waters include Badoit, Gerolsteiner, Wattwiller, Ferrarelle, and Borsec.

Perrier has a unique carbonation story. The water is distinguished by its natural carbonation, which comes from volcanic gases in the rock near the source. But as international demand for Perrier grew, the company improved efficiency by capturing the water and the carbonic gas separately. The two substances are taken from the same geological formation, but they are extracted at different depths; the gas is then filtered before being added to the water. When you open a bottle of Perrier, the level of carbonation matches that found at the spring exactly.

ARTIFICIAL CARBONATION

Joseph Priestley discovered a way to carbonate water by placing a bowl of water above a vat of fermenting beer, which gave off carbon dioxide that was then absorbed by the water. His paper "Impregnating Water with Fixed Air" was published in 1772.

At about the same time, Swedish professor Torbern Bergman came up with another carbonation method, this time using sulphuric acid and chalk. He was inspired by the springs from which water emerges naturally carbonated.

Current carbonation techniques involve pressurizing carbon dioxide before adding it to the water—the pressure increases the amount of carbon dioxide that will dissolve. Opening the bottle of water releases pressure, allowing the carbon dioxide to form bubbles that hadn't previously been visible.

The size, spacing, and quantity of bubbles in carbonated water is governed by the amount of carbon dioxide added to it. Most artifically carbonated waters have 1 to 10 mg/l of carbon dioxide.

VIRGINALITY

Virginality indicates how protected a water is from its surroundings. It is determined by the water's level of nitrate, an inorganic compound made up of one nitrogen atom and three oxygen atoms. Nitrate is easily carried through soil by water. The substance can leach into the ground below the root zone through heavy rainfall or irrigation, and it may subsequently find its way into groundwater. In its natural state, water has less than 1 mg/l of nitrate; higher levels typically reveal a compromised water. This contamination may come from fertilizer, animal waste products, decaying plant matter, septic tanks, or sewage treatment systems. Only testing can determine nitrate levels in water, as nitrate has no taste, odor, or color.

The ability of blood to carry oxygen throughout the body may be impaired by very high nitrate contamination in drinking water; this may case methemoglobinemia (also known as blue baby syndrome). Cancer, disruption of thyroid function, birth defects, and miscarriages are other health risks posed by high levels of nitrate.

The World Health Organization recommends that exposure to nitrate should not exceed 50 mg/l for short periods. In the United States, drinking water may not contain more than 10 mg/l of nitrate, a level determined by a study in 1951 of infants suffering from blue baby syndrome.

I use the following system of icons to describe the Virginality of bottled water:

SUPERIOR	♦♦♦♦♦	0–1 mg/l
VERY GOOD	♦♦♦♦	1–4 mg/l
GOOD	♦♦♦	4–7 mg/l
ACCEPTABLE	♦♦	7–10 mg/l
POTABLE	♦	10–50 mg/l

Distillation, reverse osmosis, and ion exchange can each remove nitrate from water; several manufacturers offer equipment to apply these techniques to home drinking water. Nitrate is not removed by standard water softeners or filters, including carbon adsorption filters, and boiling water actually increases the concentration of nitrate.

VINTAGE

Wine needs time to smooth out its tannin structure, but the quality of water is not determined by its age. Vintage does influence water, however. Very young waters like Hawaiian Springs and bottled rain-waters don't have much time to absorb minerals, so they tend to have low TDS levels and hence light, clean tastes.

Old water may feel more substantial, but Trinity and Fiji prove there are old waters with low levels of mineral content. The age of a water is less important than the local geology.

The age of bottled waters should be noted, though, as an enjoy-able part of their backstories, which add to the epicurean pleasure. Rain that fell when Balboa discovered the Pacific Ocean more than 450 years ago is in the Fiji water you might drink today. Bottled rainwaters such as Cloud Juice, on the other hand, may be less than one week old.

THE FINEWATERS BALANCE

With the growing popularity of bottled water, the FineWaters Balance provides a scale to define the differences between various bottled waters based on carbonation levels. It is designed to be an easily understood standard for restaurants and connoisseurs.

The FineWaters Balance helps water drinkers appreciate the difference between, for example, the large, loud bubbles of a sparkling Perrier or Ty Nant and the effervescent, small bubbles of Badoit.

It's important to note that there is no explicit or implied scale of quality associated with the FineWaters Balance. It merely compares the waters, and it is my way of pointing out the differences that allow bottled waters to be savored and fully enjoyed.

 STILL

Still waters—those that have no carbonation—are preferred by sixty-five percent of Americans when eating. The Spanish share this preference, whereas sparkling waters are favored in Italy. Still water is perfect with any food, but a little variety can go a long way. With Still waters, we can engage in a dialogue about sources and minerality and focus on the differences in Still waters based on their terroirs.

It is important to resist the temptation to pour Still water over ice—especially ice made with tap water. If you prefer your bottled water with ice, for full enjoyment make sure the ice is made with the same water.

Recommended Serving Temperature	54°F (12°C)
Carbonation	0 mg/l

EFFERVESCENT

Effervescent waters are an epicurean surprise to many. These sophisticated waters, with the smallest possible bubbles, straddle a line between Still and Light sparkling waters. In some instances these waters lose their "sparkle" very quickly, and some are almost still. Many naturally carbonated waters (such as Badoit, Wattwiller, and Ferrarelle) fall into this category.

Drinking water that is almost flat but has a hint of carbonation (and thus a hint of mouthfeel) offers a new sensation to many people. Use this element of surprise to contrast or support a dish with a water pairing.

Recommended Serving Temperature	56°F (13°C)
Carbonation	0–2.5 mg/l

LIGHT

These waters draw attention. Many people who claim they don't like sparkling water at all love Light sparkling waters. If you are serving a dish with a subtle mouthfeel—for example, a perfectly pan-seared fish—a Light sparkling water would be a perfect choice. It gives texture but does not overpower the presentation.

Recommended Serving Temperature	58°F (14°C)
Carbonation	2.5–5 mg/l

CLASSIC

Classic is what most people think of when they talk about a sparkling water. Many high mineral content waters fall into this category.

Classic waters are the workhorses of food and water pairing. Their mouthfeel matches many dishes perfectly, which makes them a safe bet. Classic waters are also perfect for mixed drinks, especially wine spritzers. In selecting specific Classic waters to pair with food, note the mineral content. A Classic water with a low TDS is a good choice for mixed drinks, while one with a higher TDS would be the perfect choice with steak.

Recommended Serving Temperature	60°F (16°C)
Carbonation	5–7.5 mg/l

BOLD

Expect bold, large, and loud bubbles. Bold waters sometimes create a "fireworks in your mouth" kind of feeling. The spacing between bubbles creates significant differences among various brands of bottled water. Some waters feel fizzy, whereas others are bold in a silent way. Served too cold, the bubbles can be overwhelming. (If people say they don't like sparkling water, this is usually what they mean.) Served closer to room temperature, the bubbles calm down. You can also use a spoon to stir the water to reduce the effect of the carbonation; opening the bottle and allowing the water to breathe will also reduce some of the effect, if desired.

Careful matching with food is required if Bold waters are to be enjoyed while dining. The strong sensation created by the large bubbles can distract from subtle foods or those with little or no mouthfeel. On the other hand, the bubbles can sometimes be used to contrast with subtle foods and give them texture. Bold waters are perfect at the beginning of a meal, preferably with crispy appetizers.

Recommended Serving Temperature	62°F (17°C)
Carbonation	>7.5 mg/l

BOTTLED WATER ETIQUETTE

MATCHING WATER WITH FOOD

Mouthfeel is the most important of the factors guiding the way bottled water is matched with food. Mineral content and acidity play more minor roles.

MATCHING WITH MOUTHFEEL

Use the FineWaters Balance to establish a progression in multiple-course meals and to match or contrast the water with the mouthfeel of the dish.

One of the prime joys of matching water and food—and one of the true marks of water connoisseurship—is changing waters for each course, developing a progression of waters to guide you through the meal. Drinking a different water for each course highlights their subtle differences, and the progression adds enormously to the dining experience. If your favorite restaurant does not offer more than one water, ask them to consider adding more options.

For a five-course dinner, a good water progression might look like this:

- Hors d'oeuvre: Bold or Classic. This is much like having a taste of champagne—it draws attention and is bubbly and loud.
- Salad: Effervescent. A nice contrast with the previous water but not entirely without bubbles.
- First course (light seafood, for example): Still. You'll notice the absence of bubbles and focus on the water.
- Second course (poultry, for example): Effervescent or Light. Reintroduce some mouthfeel and match the water with the texture of the course.
- Main course (red meat, for example): Light or Classic. Match it with the texture of the course.
- Dessert: Still or Effervescent.

Try these simple examples to elevate drinking water to an experience. To go further, consider the principles of complement and contrast.

Sometimes contrasting the texture of the food allows for enhanced pleasures. Raw oysters come to mind: These would go perfectly well with a Still water but might be more enjoyable with a Light sparkling water, which would provide additional sensation in the mouth. The same rule applies to "fusion" sushi or sashimi dishes, especially when they have some spiciness. A spicy tuna tartar is another good example of a food that asks for a contrasting Light to Classic water. Other foods that do well with contrasting waters are hot and spicy foods, desserts, sweets, and cheeses. Many dishes can benefit from a water contrast—I encourage you to experiment and find new sensations.

MATCHING WITH MINERAL CONTENT

The amount of total dissolved solids is, after mouthfeel, the second most important factor in pairing water with food. The TDS in water ranges from the absolute 0 of distilled water (such as Le Bleu) to a

SAMPLE MENU

Carbonation or its absence, together with the size, amount, and distribution of bubbles, makes a significant contribution to the mouthfeel of water and thus should be your prime focus when matching water and food. The FineWaters Balance gives you a good indication of mouthfeel. Here's a sample menu of how a meal might work with water:

- A salad of seasonal vegetables and fruit with shaved truffles and a truffled sherry vinaigrette is a good example of a salad that would be perfect with an Effervescent water.
- A first course of seafood, like sablefish with lobster pomme fourchette and a lobster emulsion, suggests a Still water. This water won't overpower the subtleness of the fish-lobster combination.
- Roast breast of squab on a savory crouton with beets, long beans, and pistachios, a good example of a second (poultry) course, calls for an Effervescent or Light water to contrast the texture, especially if the squab is a little bit crispy.
- Strip loin of beef with seared foie gras, fondant potatoes, baby spinach, and wild mushrooms might have a very similar texture to the previous course, but taking the progression of water into account, a Light or Classic water seems to be a perfect match for this main course.
- Desserts usually call for a "soft, sweet" Still water or an Effervescent if some texture in the water is called for.

Credit for menu: Patina Restaurant, Los Angeles, 2002

whopping 13,298 mg/l for Donat Mg, a curative from Slovenia that is a meal in itself.

The borders of TDS categories are fluid, and sometimes the actual mineral composition of the waters plays a significant role in the group designation. Keep that in mind when using the following taste guidelines to pair water with food:

Super Low TDS	0–50 mg/l	very light and neutral taste
Low TDS	50–250 mg/l	clean, soft, and neutral taste
Medium TDS	250–800 mg/l	classic mineral water taste
High TDS	800–1,500 mg/l	more substance
Very High TDS	1,500–3,000 mg/l	substantial feel
	>3,000 mg/l	very distinct character and taste

MATCHING WITH pH FACTOR

Most of the food we eat is acidic, ranging from a pH of 2.4 for cranberry sauce to 7.2 for spinach, shrimp, and certain cheeses. Use the taste of the water as influenced by pH factor (sour, sweet, or bitter) to complement or contrast with the taste of the dish. The pH level is only a minor component in pairing water with food, though, and it should not be overemphasized—water pairing is not a pH numbers game. I love Perrier (pH 5.46) with crisp fried oysters (pH 5.7) and Borsec (pH 6.45) with cheese (pH 7.5).

INTANGIBLES

Beyond the pure flavor considerations, you should also take intangible qualities like presentation and a water's story into account when choosing your bottled water.

The bottle plays an important role in the overall perception of the water. Since water has no notable visible characteristics of its own, the bottle has a remarkable impact on perceived value. Matching the presentation to the venue or event may have no influence on the actual taste (as any blind water tasting will tell you), but doing so can significantly enhance the experience—or be detrimental to it. Plastic or glass; minimalist or traditional design; attention grabbing or discreet; blue or transparent—bottlers offer many presentation options. Wine bottle design, on the other hand, is fairly uniform—most wineries focus all their attention on the label. With water we are lucky: Both the label and the bottle can express terroir (as is the case for Antipodes, Bling H$_2$O, and Finé).

Every good sommelier tells you a little story about the wine he or she is pouring you. Does it make the wine taste better? No. Does it make the wine feel more special and unique? Absolutely. The same is true for water: Sharing the story of the water—its source and origin, vintage, and the location and circumstances of its bottling—can contribute significantly to the overall experience.

RULES FOR BOTTLED WATER WITH FOOD ONLY

Creating a matrix matching all foods with bottled waters would be impossible, and it would surely take the fun out of experimenting with various combinations. The rules below should be taken as starting points for an exploration. Use them when water is the only beverage you are serving. (The next section describes how to choose water when you're also serving wine as the meal's primary beverage.) The percentages indicate how much weight the factor should be given in making your choice.

- The 75 Percent Rule: The mouthfeel sensation of the whole dish should be matched with the carbonation level of the water.

  The mouthfeel generated by the bubbles should be matched with the mouthfeel of the dish. Loud, big, bold bubbles overpower subtle dishes, while Still water might be too great a contrast with crispy food. Bigger bubbles would stand up better to the mouthfeel of such a dish.

An alternative epicurean pleasure can be achieved by carefully contrasting the mouthfeel of a dish with a water's carbonation. Sushi with an Effervescent or even Light carbonated water is a perfect example.

• **The 20 Percent Rule:** The dominant food items of the dish should be matched with the mineral content of the water.

Low TDS waters have a light, sometimes crisp, perception, while higher TDS levels give the water some weight and substance. High levels of sodium (salt), bicarbonate, and silica (or their absence) can also have some impact on the perception of the water. Use sodium-free water with caviar or water with a high bicarbonate level for cheese. Softer waters (low in calcium and magnesium) with higher silica levels can display a nice sweet softness that works well with some desserts.

• **The 5 Percent Rule:** Fine-tune the drinking experience with the water's acidity or alkalinity.

A neutral pH works well with anything. Sometimes a sweet perception is possible in waters with a slight alkalinity, while waters with a very high pH may demonstrate a very subtle bitterness, but never an unpleasant one. Try matching acidic water with fatty food or seafood. The contribution that pH factor makes to food and water matching is easily overrated—only on the outer ranges of the spectrum (less than 5 or more than 10) does it play a more significant role.

• Don't forget to consider the water's bottle and backstory, too.

MATCHING TABLE: WATER AND FOOD

FOOD	CARBONATION (FWB, 75%)	MINERALITY (20%)	ORIENTATION (5%)
MEAT			
BEEF			
Grilled/seared	Classic	High	Alkaline
Braised	Effervescent	Medium	Neutral
VEAL			
Grilled/seared	Light	Medium	Hint of Sweet
Braised	Still	Medium	Hint of Sweet
PORK			
Grilled/seared	Light	Medium	Neutral
Braised	Still	Medium	Neutral
LAMB			
Grilled/seared	Classic	Very High	Alkaline
Braised	Effervescent	Very High	Alkaline
GAME			
Grilled/seared	Classic	Very High	Alkaline
Braised	Effervescent	Very High	Alkaline
POULTRY			
CHICKEN			
Fried	Bold	Medium	Acidic
Roasted	Classic	Medium	Acidic
Seared/sautéed	Still	Medium	Neutral
OTHER POULTRY			
Duck	Still	High	Neutral
Game	Effervescent	Very High	Alkaline
Turkey	Classic	High	Neutral
Foie gras	Effervescent	Low	Acidic

SEAFOOD

White fish	Still	Super Low	Neutral
Dark fish	Still	Low	Neutral
Smoked fish	Effervescent	Low	Acidic
Clams & mussels	Still	Super Low	Acidic
Crab	Still	Low	Neutral
Lobster	Still	Super Low	Neutral
Scallops	Still	Low	Neutral
Shrimp (fried)	Classic	Low	Acidic
Caviar	Still/Effervescent*	Super Low	Neutral

CHEESE

Hard	Effervescent	High	Neutral
Soft	Still	Low	Hint of Sweet
Blue	Light	Medium	Alkaline

*Still or Effervescent water served with caviar should be low in sodium.

RULES FOR BOTTLED WATER WITH FOOD AND WINE

If water is consumed alongside wine, different considerations apply: The water now plays a secondary role and needs to be matched with the wine, not the food. This is very important—you don't want water and wine competing with each other for attention.

If you drink carefully matched wine with your dish, only still water is appropriate—a clear distinction between main character (wine) and supporting cast (water) is necessary. But there is a slight difference between red and white wine: With white wine, choose water with a low mineral content and a neutral pH; red wine demands water with a medium to high mineral content and a neutral pH.

The water should have a slightly higher temperature than the wine to prevent taking attention away from the wine. Think about stemware, too—most reputable producers of wineglass series offer water glasses that complement the wineglasses.

DRINKING TEMPERATURE

For centuries, humans have been drinking water at the natural temperature of its source or storage facility. Only recently have we begun manipulating water's temperature.

The temperature of most underground cellars where wine is traditionally stored is about 55 degrees Fahrenheit (13°C). There is nothing fundamentally wrong with consuming any wine at this temperature, but most wine aficionados will agree that manipulating the temperature can enhance the drinking experience. You may like to serve your champagne at a refreshing 42 degrees Fahrenheit (6°C) and your bordeaux closer to 64 degrees Fahrenheit (18°C), for example. The narrow range of temperatures between these endpoints serves the whole spectrum of wines, with all its intricate tastes and aromas, and is the base for an endlessly evolving dialogue of wine and food pairings.

Curiously, 55 degrees Fahrenheit is also the temperature of many springs or wells. The temperature similarity between cellars and springs shouldn't be surprising, though, given that both are located underground.

Serving all waters at the same temperature, let's say 55 degrees Fahrenheit, will nicely show their differences. A slight increase in temperature will have a calming effect on waters with larger, louder bubbles. In general, the colder the water, the more focused it will be. Water can be served at almost any temperature, but knowing how to manipulate temperature will allow you to better pair the waters with food and establish a true epicurean dialogue.

These are the temperatures I generally recommend for serving water:

CARBONATION LEVEL	TEMPERATURE
STILL	54°F (12°C)
EFFERVESCENT	56°F (13°C)
LIGHT	58°F (14°C)
CLASSIC	60°F (16°C)
BOLD	62°F (17°C)

ICE

The American fascination with ice in soft drinks and water is one of the first things to strike many visitors to the United States. Even sparkling water is not spared this cruel treatment. I may not be able to change the use of ice in soft drinks, but I hope there is a chance to save bottled water from this fate.

Ice is the natural enemy of bottled water (and soft drinks for that matter). Before drinking, bottled water should be cooled to the proper temperature without ice.

As ice made from tap water melts, it dilutes the bottled water—water that has been taken from its natural source, bottled with great care, and shipped halfway around the world. There is usually nothing wrong with tap water, but it just does not belong in natural bottled water.

The troubles become apparent if you look closely at how the ice is actually produced, stored, and handled. For example, a bottle of water is usually opened at the table, but you have no idea who handled your ice and how long it has been sitting around in an open container. There is, of course, a "legitimate" use of ice in cocktails and mixed drinks, and I know there are many people who don't want to give up the additional mouthfeel of crushing ice with their teeth. The solution to the problem is to take control of your ice's supply chain. Sound complicated? It's actually very simple: Source it yourself, or use a source you trust.

ICE CUBE TRAYS

At home, just fill your ice cube tray with the bottled water you plan to drink. This makes the ice cubes a little bit more expensive, but it is worth the cost. Choose these cubes if you must have ice in your water, or you can use them for making cocktails.

For example, you may have spent a fortune on the latest and greatest vodka for your martini, but then you use ice cubes made of tap water to mix the drink. Try freezing a high-end water with a neutral pH and a low TDS in some designer ice cube trays. The taste will be improved, and your guests will be impressed.

Ice cubes do shrink in their trays, especially in frost-free refrigerators, which are often very dry—about twenty percent relative humidity. The evaporation phenomenon is called sublimation; fill the tray right to the top to minimize its effects.

If you want transparent ice cubes, use distilled water (such as Le Bleu) that is not aerated. You will have to experiment with the freezing rate. Clear ice usually does not stay that way for long.

DRINK ICE

Some innovative bottled water companies, such as Diamond Ice, have begun offering single-use ice cube trays filled at the source. All you have to do is put these prefilled trays, called drink ice, into the freezer.

When you open a tray of drink ice, you can be sure it's the first time the ice has encountered the air since it left the clean room in which the tray was filled. Drink ice is much too expensive to fill your cooler with, but I hope it will become a standard in bars and restaurants for mixed drinks and cocktails.

I look forward to the time when people can select not only the vodka for their martini, but also the ice. "Make this an Antipodes Ketel One Martini with two olives, please."

STEMWARE

The sorry state of the "glass culture" surrounding bottled water is a sure sign that the best of the bottled water trend is yet to come. Many fine restaurants overlook the emerging trend and fail to provide proper water glasses—water, it quickly becomes clear, is usually an afterthought. I don't mind paying eight dollars for a bottle of water, but I want it served in an appropriate glass. Instead, I've been served water in all possible vessels, from a heavy whiskey tumbler to a long highball glass and the dreaded lemonade glass.

A wide variety of wineglasses are also often used as water glasses. This is unfortunate, as it confuses the waiters and you have to constantly remind them not to pour wine into your "water glass."

I usually consider myself lucky if I get a water goblet (a glass with a base and stem), but unfortunately these are usually heavy glass and look like second-class citizens of the table setting. There are some nice water goblets (also sometimes called mineral water glasses) available from manufacturers like Riedel, Spiegelau, and others. These are usually shorter than the wineglasses they're designed to be set with—they are cast in a supporting role and draw no attention. Usually made of lead crystal by machine, the glasses are reasonably priced and dishwasher safe. If you drink wine with the meal, these glasses are perfect for the accompanying water.

But if water is your main drink with a meal, you also need appropriate glassware—and it isn't a water goblet. Toasting with a water goblet just looks silly. Luckily, leading manufacturers produce other special glasses for water. Unfortunately, these glasses seldom make it into restaurants and are rarely seen in private dining settings. Nevertheless, this is the way to go if you like to experience fine bottled water.

The companies that design these water glasses take different approaches. Most of the glasses in this category are expensive, hand-blown lead crystal, and you would probably not trust your dishwasher to clean them. They are meant to blend into the overall design and shape of the wineglass series they are part of—the tall glasses are similar in shape to white-wine glasses. Sometimes the design is identical to the wineglass but made out of cobalt blue glass. A cobalt glass is good if you're drinking both water and wine (and a water goblet doesn't do it for you), but if you drink only water or are switching water between courses, colored glass is not necessary.

Riedel took a slightly different approach with its renowned Sommeliers series. These glasses have for years tried to establish themselves not as variations on wineglasses but as true water glasses, with a unique, straight shape.

In the case of both the Riedel glasses and more wineglass-inspired glassware, your first impression will be the tactile sensation of a fine, hand-blown glass. It is tall and thin, and you can feel the weight of the water. The visual impact is commanding: These are usually the tallest glasses on the table.

There are, of course, many casual dining situations in which a water glass as described above would be out of place, and even a water goblet might be a little bit too formal. Such occasions require a water tumbler—a simple, flat-bottomed glass with no foot or stem. These tumblers come in different shapes, colors, and patterns and are usually machine made out of sturdy glass. They have a solid feeling and are perfect for barbeques or casual picnics.

GLASS OR PLASTIC?

About 100 BCE, Syrians invented the glass bottle by blowing molten glass through a tube. Until mass production became possible, glass bottles were expensive, so Apollinaris and other waters were sold in earthen jars.

Always choose glass if possible—it just has a nicer feel and looks more substantial. I've found no evidence of any taste difference between glass and plastic, but I keep looking. If you want to drink the still water from an ugly plastic bottle in an epicurean context, decant it or put the bottle into a sleeve.

For high-end bottled waters, the glass bottle is a must. The bottles—though sometimes over designed and under functional, as in the case of Voss (the water's slim bottle is easily jostled)—are the most visible aspect of a water brand. While some bottlers only put their water in glass, other brands establish a distinct identity in both glass and plastic (Ty Nant, for example). Lately, some bottlers that have previously only bottled in PET are moving to glass in order to capture a higher market segment through sales in restaurants and hotels. Perrier, on the other hand, departed in 2001 from its well-known glass bottle by introducing a half-liter PET bottle.

> When you see the number 1 in the recycling arrows on the bottom of a drink bottle or jar of peanut butter, that package has been made with polyethylene terephthalate, or PET. This type of polyester is a strong, transparent plastic resin that keeps its shape even when subjected to temperature changes. PET is also fairly cheap to produce, doesn't shatter like glass, and is lightweight and recyclable.

CAPS

Cap style is an issue of presentation rather than taste. In an epicurean setting, I like the tradition of crown caps and cork, but the convenience of a screw top can't be beat for resealing sparkling water bottles.

The earliest bottle stoppers were made from cork or wood, and even today, most wine bottles are sealed with a cork. In 1856, a screw cap with a cork disk was invented to seal glass jars, and the bottle cap we're familiar with today first appeared in 1890. The single-use, removable "crown cork" cap—so called because it was shaped much like the British queen's crown—was invented by William Painter. As mass production of glass bottles began in the early twentieth century, usage of of crown caps increased—within twenty years they sealed almost all bottles produced. The crown cork is still used for bottled water, especially by traditional bottlers in Europe.

Crown caps were lined with plastic rather than cork beginning in the 1960s, when synthetics became more economically feasible. Today, most water bottles (glass and plastic) are sealed with pilfer-proof (PP) screw caps made from aluminum and plastic.

While the wine industry has begun to adopt screw caps to overcome the three to five percent spoilage when using natural cork, some adventurous bottled water companies are reintroducing the cork (or

URBAN LEGENDS ABOUT PLASTIC BOTTLES

"Avoid freezing water in plastic bottles to prevent exposure to carcinogenic dioxins."

Scientists agree that there are no dioxins in plastics. Furthermore, cold temperatures actually inhibit the diffusion of chemicals.

"Reusing plastic water bottles (PET) can cause them to break down into carcinogenic compounds (such as diethylhydroxylamine, or DEHA)."

The IBWA says this belief comes from nothing more than someone's master's thesis, which itself states that DEHA is not considered a carcinogen by government authorities. PET doesn't contain or decompose into DEHA, which the FDA has approved for contact with food. But you should always wash and dry bottles thoroughly before reusing them to prevent the spread of bacteria.

artificial cork substitutes). Nothing compares to opening a fine bottle of water with a corkscrew—but there is potential for spoilage with natural cork. Molds and chlorine bleach (which is used when corks are made) react inside corks to produce trichloroanisole (TCA), which is responsible for the spoilage. Cork has not been used with bottled water long enough to determine if the water will be spoiled by this chemical as wine is.

STORAGE AND SHELF LIFE

Under optimal conditions, bottled water has an indefinite shelf life. Even so, it is date stamped for two years in the United States. This is mainly for stock rotation purposes—it does not imply that the product is compromised after that date. As long as bottled water is packaged in accordance with governmental regulations and good manufacturing practices, you shouldn't have to worry about the product expiring.

However, long-term storage of bottled water may cause aesthetic defects, such as off odor and taste. The International Bottled Water Association (IBWA) recommends storing bottled water no higher than room temperature in an unopened container, away from direct sunlight, and separated from chemicals such as gasoline or paint thinner. I keep my collection in the wine cellar at about 55 degrees Fahrenheit (13°C).

DECANTING WATER

This may sound ridiculous, but decanting water makes sense under certain circumstances. Some very nice and special waters with a lot of terroir come in ugly commodity PET or, even worse, sports bottles. You probably don't want to see these bottles at an epicurean table, as they deflate the value of the water and maybe even the event.

In these cases, decant still water into a jug and serve it that way. Sparkling water should not be decanted, as this alters the carbonation of the water significantly.

Some bottlers, such as Fiji and 1 Litre, want to promote the use of their plastic bottles in more formal settings, so they offer attractive metal or ceramic sleeves. Because they keep the water in the original bottle, such sleeves do not alter the carbonation level.

HOW TO CONDUCT A WATER TASTING

A tasting provides the best introduction to the surprising richness of epicurean experiences with water. Here are directions for conducting your own. I recommend that, at the beginning, it not be conducted blind: A water tasting should be fun—more of an introduction to the differences in bottled waters than a hardcore blind tasting, which can be intimidating.

As the host, you should provide information on all the waters and let people enjoy the tactile experience of handling the bottle. Here are a few guidelines:

- Buy as many waters as possible from each of the five FineWaters Balance categories—Still, Effervescent, Light, Classic, and Bold. One bottle is enough for six to eight people. You should have at least ten waters—fifteen is a better number (two to three in each category). Within each of the categories, try to find waters with different TDS levels, sources (spring water or rainwater), or countries or regions of origin.
- Chill all the waters to about 55 degrees Fahrenheit (13°C) to nicely showcase the differences in the waters. Make sure they stay at the same temperature throughout the tasting—otherwise their qualities (or the perception of them) will change.
- You will need two to three proper water glasses per person. Ideally, have each flight in the glasses at the same time.
- Start with Still and work your way through the levels up to Bold.
- You can swallow, but have a bucket ready for emptying glasses.

- Sometimes it's fun to have "pure H_2O" available to calibrate your palate. Le Bleu distilled water is one good choice that is widely available.
- Serve bread or crackers, but not salty food.
- Make notes if you wish, describing how the water feels (short, long, focused, wide, and so forth).

Because the waters vary significantly in mineral content, mouthfeel, and other characteristics, it will be hard to pick a "best water." Instead, think of foods that would be good complements to particular waters.

BOTTLED WATER: A NATURAL HANGOVER FIGHTER

Hangovers are caused by dehydration. The headache, nausea, and dry mouth of overindulgence occur when alcohol has deprived your body of the water it needs. Drinking water restores your fluid levels, speeds up the metabolization of alcohol, and flushes out toxins.

Treat yourself and your guests to hangover-fighting bottled water the next time you entertain. You can start drinking water as soon as you get out of bed and keep drinking throughout the day. I think it's fun to fend off hangovers with three bottles of fine water, using quality stemware during the party. A selection of three different waters allows your guests to drink those that pair well with the wine or hard liquor sure to be flowing. Any water will do, but helping guests enjoy the rehydration process makes them more likely to drink enough to combat a hangover. Your guests will appreciate your efforts and surely thank you the next morning.

| PART II |

DIRECTORY OF WATERS

G enerating a list of all the bottled waters available in the world today would be nearly impossible. I estimate the total number of bottled water brands available worldwide to be about three thousand. With around six hundred brands, Italy has not only the highest number of bottled waters, but also the highest consumption, with a whopping 50 gallons (189 l) per capita annually. Germany and Japan each offer around 450 brands, and in France you find about two hundred brands. Those four countries alone produce a little more than half of the bottled water brands available on the market today. The waters of Japan and Germany are not widely distributed in the United States, so Italy and France are really the world's superpowers of bottled water. But many very interesting waters are available from almost every corner of the world.

As you can imagine, it was very hard to decide which waters to include in this book's small selection of one hundred. The waters included should not be considered the best waters in the world, but rather a very personal "favorites list" of one hundred very interesting waters that also have reasonable availability. If you see a bottled water I haven't covered that looks interesting, buy it and give it a try. Chances are it's very good water, and this book will give you the tools to judge for yourself—my selection of waters is intended as an educational resource rather than a "best of" list.

As a result, this book has no overall numeric rating system for water—I would rather let you decide. The influential wine-rating scale developed by Robert Parker and *Wine Spectator* has a maximum of 100 for the very best wines; most are rated between 80 and 94. Such a system is useful to some extent, but it can lead to what people in the wine industry call "shopping by numbers": Consumers use the rating system as the almost exclusive criteria for purchasing wine, thinking a 92 must be much better then a 89—which it is not. The 89 is different from the 92, and you might even like the lower number more.

For each water, this book offers a list of properties (carbonation, minerality, hardness, orientation, virginality, and vintage) along with a general description of the source and the water's background. I also try to characterize the waters with my personal comments. These are my own tastes and opinions; you may find that you feel different. Let the book guide your intelligent attention.

Here is a summary of the categories and descriptions used for the individual waters:

Carbonation (FineWaters Balance)

STILL	0 mg/l carbonation
EFFERVESCENT	0–2.5 mg/l
LIGHT	2.5–5 mg/l
CLASSIC	5–7.5 mg/l
BOLD	>7.5 mg/l

Minerality (TDS)

SUPER LOW	0–50 mg/l total dissolved solids
LOW	50–250 mg/l
MEDIUM	250–800 mg/l
HIGH	800–1,500 mg/l
VERY HIGH	>1,500 mg/l

Orientation (pH)

ACIDIC	pH 5–6.7
NEUTRAL	6.7–7.3
HINT OF SWEET	7.3–7.8
ALKALINE	7.8–10

Hardness (Calcium and Magnesium)

SOFT	0–17.1 mg/l hardness
SLIGHTLY HARD	17.1–60 mg/l
MODERATELY HARD	60–120 mg/l
HARD	120–180 mg/l
VERY HARD	>180 mg/l

Virginality (Nitrate)

SUPERIOR	◆◆◆◆◆	0–1 mg/l nitrate
VERY GOOD	◆◆◆◆	1–4 mg/l
GOOD	◆◆◆	4–7 mg/l
ACCEPTABLE	◆◆	7–10 mg/l
POTABLE	◆	10–50 mg/l

NOTE: If a number falls on the borderline of two ranges, use the lesser level—for example, a virginality of 4 mg/l would be considered Very Good, while anything more than 4 mg/l would be Good. Mathematically, the ranges would be represented as $x > $ mg/l $ \leq y$, where x is the lower end of the range and y the upper end.

ANTIPODES

Established 2003

STILL   LIGHT

Antipodes comes from a pristine source and is a soft, low mineral content, artificially carbonated water with a neutral taste. The clean, modern bottle shows elegance as well as local character— it's modeled after the traditional New Zealand sherry or beer bottle. Antipodes is sold in the hospitality and restaurant industry only.

Antipodes water spends fifty years under pressure in an aquifer 500 to 1,000 feet (150–305 m) below the earth, where an ignimbrite substratum acts as a natural filter. The Rotoma Hills, where rainwater that replenishes the aquifer falls, is free of industry and has a population density of not even one person per 250 acres (100 hectares).

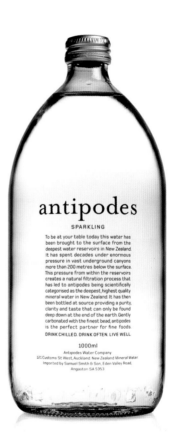

Otakiri, Whakatane,
New Zealand

CARBONATION artificial **TDS** 120 mg/l **HARDNESS** 15 mg/l
pH 6.9 **NITRATE** <1 mg/l **CALCIUM** 3 mg/l **MAGNESIUM** 0 mg/l
SODIUM 12 mg/l **POTASSIUM** 3.5 mg/l **SILICA** 76 mg/l
BICARBONATE 37 mg/l **SULFATES** 3 mg/l **CHLORIDES** 0 mg/l

VIRGINALITY: ♦ ♦ ♦ ♦ ♦
REGION: Bay of Plenty, North Island
SOURCE: Artesian
MINERALITY: Low
HARDNESS: Soft
ORIENTATION: Neutral
VINTAGE: 50 years

APOLLINARIS

Established 1892

STILL | CLASSIC

A rare, naturally carbonated sparkling water with very high mineral content and sufficient carbonation for a Classic designation. The natural carbonation makes this water very special, and it is best enjoyed pure. Not the perfect water for mixing drinks due to its high mineral content.

The Eifel region's volcanic activity enriches Apollinaris with minerals, and the water is naturally carbonated by carbon dioxide given off by the magma. The water of Eifel has been valued as a luxury drink since Roman times, when it was distributed across the empire's territory in clay jugs. Later, Apollinaris sold its water in earthen jars before moving to the glass bottles we know today.

Bad Neuenahr-Ahrweiler, GERMANY

CARBONATION 7.5 mg/l natural TDS 1,600 mg/l HARDNESS 783 mg/l pH 5.8 NITRATE 3 mg/l CALCIUM 100 mg/l MAGNESIUM 130 mg/l SODIUM 410 mg/l POTASSIUM 20 mg/l BICARBONATE 1,810 mg/l SULFATES 80 mg/l CHLORIDES 100 mg/l

VIRGINALITY: ◆ ◆ ◆ ◆
REGION: Eifel
SOURCE: Spring at 359 feet (109 m)
MINERALITY: Very High
HARDNESS: Very Hard
ORIENTATION: Acidic

AQUA PACIFIC

Established 1999

STILL

Very similar to Fiji water, Aqua Pacific is a low mineral content water, high in silica and bicarbonate (which is beneficial for digestion) with a smooth and possible sweet perception. The water has an extremely low nitrate level, indicating a pristine, unspoiled source.

Rain that falls in the highlands of Nadi will spend hundreds of years trickling though (and being filtered by) volcanic rock on its way to the artesian aquifer used as the source of Aqua Pacific. Tapping the aquifer releases its pressure, which then forces the water up the well and to the surface, where the bottler performs additional filtration, removing particles larger than 0.2 microns, and ozonates the water.

Nausori Highlands,
Fiji

TDS 250 mg/l **HARDNESS** 147 mg/l **pH** 7.5 **NITRATE** 0.1 mg/l **CALCIUM** 33 mg/l **MAGNESIUM** 16 mg/l **SODIUM** 10 mg/l **POTASSIUM** 1 mg/l **SILICA** 61 mg/l **BICARBONATE** 167 mg/l **CHLORIDES** 7 mg/l

VIRGINALITY: ♦ ♦ ♦ ♦ ♦

REGION: Nadi, Viti Levu

SOURCE: Artesian at 279 feet (85 m)

MINERALITY: Low

HARDNESS: Hard

ORIENTATION: Hint of Sweet

VINTAGE: 500 years

BADOIT

Established 1837

EFFERVESCENT

Badoit is a substantial water, but despite the high amount of minerals, it has a very light taste. This is water for people who say they don't like sparkling mineral water—the effervescent small and very fine bubbles give a nice structure to the water. The high level of bicarbonate is beneficial for digestion.

A naturally carbonated mineral water, Badoit is often paired with fine cuisine and wine in top French restaurants, leading some to call it "the gourmet's mineral water." Neither the sodium bicarbonate nor the fluoride is removed after the water makes its 1,640-foot (500 m) journey up a granite fissure, and the light sparkle is left intact. Only about 69 million gallons (260 million l) are bottled each year, so this is a rare water.

St. Galmier,
France

CARBONATION 2.5 mg/l natural TDS 1,200 mg/l HARDNESS 815 mg/l pH 6 NITRATE NA CALCIUM 190 mg/l MAGNESIUM 85 mg/l SODIUM 150 mg/l POTASSIUM 10 mg/l SILICA 5 mg/l BICARBONATE 1,300 mg/l SULFATES 40 mg/l CHLORIDES 40 mg/l

VIRGINALITY: Not Available

REGION: Massif Central

SOURCE: Spring

MINERALITY: High

HARDNESS: Very Hard

ORIENTATION: Acidic

BERNINA

Established 1960

STILL

A super low mineral content, neutral pH water from an Alpine source, Bernina is ideal for any subtle dishes that require a low TDS water.

Bernina is only one of many springs in Piuro, which is about an hour and a half away from Italy's border with Switzerland. The other springs include Aurosina, Frisia, and Rovani. Levissima, a water similar to Bernina (but with slightly more minerality), also comes from the same valley.

Piuro,
ITALY

TDS 36 mg/l HARDNESS 22 mg/l pH 7.1 NITRATE <1 mg/l
CALCIUM 8 mg/l MAGNESIUM 1 mg/l SODIUM 1 mg/l
POTASSIUM 1 mg/l SILICA 5 mg/l BICARBONATE 20 mg/l
SULFATES 6 mg/l CHLORIDES 1 mg/l

VIRGINALITY: ♦ ♦ ♦ ♦
REGION: Sondrio
SOURCE: Spring at 2,050 feet (625 m)
MINERALITY: Super Low
HARDNESS: Slightly Hard
ORIENTATION: Neutral

BLING H$_2$O

ESTABLISHED 2005

STILL

Bling H$_2$O brings low TDS water from the Great Smoky Mountains of Tennessee to star-studded events like the MTV Video Music Awards and the Emmys. The company aims at the market for luxury water.

Hollywood writer and producer Kevin G. Boyd noticed that waters carried by celebrities were becoming status symbols on set, but he sensed a gap in the market for water that would show off a special something extra. He created Bling H$_2$O—sold in limited-edition bottles sealed with a cork and decorated by hand with Swarovski crystals—to stand out from the crowd.

Chestnut Hill,
Dandridge, USA

TDS 140 mg/l HARDNESS 27 mg/l pH 7.66 NITRATE 0.38 mg/l MAGNESIUM 6.8 mg/l SODIUM 1.5 mg/l POTASSIUM 1.2 mg/l BICARBONATE 100 mg/l SULFATES 8.3 mg/l CHLORIDES 1.2 mg/l

VIRGINALITY: ♦ ♦ ♦ ♦ ♦
REGION: Tennessee
SOURCE: Spring
MINERALITY: Low
HARDNESS: Hard
ORIENTATION: Hint of Sweet

BORSEC

An award-winning water, Borsec has fine, small bubbles and a distinct aftertaste. I love it with cheese, especially hard varieties. The high level of bicarbonate is beneficial for digestion.

A naturally occurring spring and two artificial wells bring Borsec water up from a clay-covered aquifer of limestone and dolomite. It became well-known in the sixteenth century, when wood casks of the water were brought to the Transylvanian royal court. Rumors of Borsec's healing powers spread in the eighteenth century. The water was believed to be Austrian emperor Franz Josef's personal water of choice, and he bestowed upon Borsec the title "Queen of Mineral Waters."

Borsec Spa,
ROMANIA

CARBONATION 3.6 mg/l natural **TDS** 1,402 mg/l **HARDNESS** 67 mg/l **pH** 6.5 **NITRATE** NA **CALCIUM** 310 mg/l **MAGNESIUM** 97 mg/l **SODIUM** 53 mg/l **POTASSIUM** 12 mg/l **BICARBONATE** 1,800 mg/l **SULFATES** 24 mg/l **CHLORIDES** 29 mg/l

VIRGINALITY: Not Available
REGION: Carpathian Region
SOURCE: Spring at 2,950 feet (900 m)
MINERALITY: High
HARDNESS: Moderately Hard
ORIENTATION: Acidic

CANAQUA

Established 2004

STILL

A great source makes great water. Canaqua is a low sodium, low mineral content water from a pristine source with nice calcium levels. I love the unique bottle with its big mouth. Expect to see more of this water worldwide, as it is rapidly becoming the "Official Water of Canada."

From a fault 1,200 feet (366 m) above sea level, in mountain bedrock, the water flows at a constant rate of 581 gallons (2,200 l) per minute. Heavy vegetation prevents contamination of the water, and the steady rate of flow indicates that rainfall and other precipitation probably have little impact.

Coghlan,
CANADA

TDS 114 mg/l HARDNESS 282 mg/l pH 8 NITRATE <1 mg/l
CALCIUM 99 mg/l MAGNESIUM 8 mg/l SODIUM 0.4 mg/l
POTASSIUM NA SILICA NA BICARBONATE NA SULFATES NA
CHLORIDES NA

VIRGINALITY: ♦ ♦ ♦ ♦ ♦
REGION: British Columbia
SOURCE: Spring at 1,200 feet (365 m)
MINERALITY: Low
HARDNESS: Very Hard
ORIENTATION: Alkaline

CAPE GRIM

ESTABLISHED 1999

STILL EFFERVESCENT

A soft, very neutral-tasting water with a super low TDS and a very good story to tell. The glass bottle makes a captivating, upscale presentation.

There are few places left in the world where air pollution is nearly nonexistent, but Cape Grim in northwest Tasmania is one of them. Clean air means unpolluted rain, which falls on the cold, remote, and rocky site of the Cape Grim Water Company for about 185 days each year. The company, which began selling water in 1999, has invested heavily in equipment to harvest this natural source of pure water.

Cape Grim,
AUSTRALIA

CARBONATION artificial TDS 5 mg/l HARDNESS 12 mg/l pH 7.3 NITRATE <1 mg/l CALCIUM 3 mg/l MAGNESIUM 1 mg/l SODIUM 7 mg/l POTASSIUM 1 mg/l SILICA <1 mg/l BICARBONATE <1 mg/l SULFATES 2 mg/l CHLORIDES <5 mg/l

VIRGINALITY: ◆ ◆ ◆ ◆ ◆

REGION: Tasmania

SOURCE: Rain

MINERALITY: Super Low

HARDNESS: Soft

ORIENTATION: Neutral

VINTAGE: 1 week

CELTIC

STILL   LIGHT   CLASSIC

Celtic, a super low mineral content water, is available in two levels of carbonation, so you can fine tune it to an epicurean event. A perfect water for mixed drinks. Celtic is sodium free.

Celts identified the spring and its healthful waters with the virtuous goddess Liese and carved her bust into the source's rock (the carving can still be seen). The Romans also appreciated the water from Vosges du Nord, which today enjoys UNESCO protection. The water gets its composition by filtering slowly through stone unique to the region, known as vosgien stone.

Vosges du Nord,
FRANCE

CARBONATION 5 mg/l, 7.5 mg/l artificial TDS 50 mg/l HARDNESS 41 mg/l pH 6.6 NITRATE 2.1 mg/l CALCIUM 10 mg/l MAGNESIUM 4 mg/l SODIUM 1 mg/l POTASSIUM 4 mg/l BICARBONATE 48 mg/l SULFATES 6 mg/l CHLO-RIDES 5 mg/l

VIRGINALITY: ◆ ◆ ◆ ◆
REGION: Vosges du Nord
SOURCE: Spring
MINERALITY: Very Low
HARDNESS: Slightly Hard
ORIENTATION: Acidic

CHATELDON

ESTABLISHED 1650

LIGHT

This water has lots of everything—very high mineral content; whopping levels of bicarbonate, calcium, and sodium; and a healthy measure of prestige and pedigree. Chateldon is also very rare: Only 700,000 bottles of this naturally sparkling water are produced each year.

Chateldon has been continuously bottled since 1650, longer than any other water. The water was known for its healthful properties even earlier. Louis XIV enjoyed it enough to employ a special group known as *les officiers du gobelet à cheval* ("mounted officers of the goblet") to bring the water to Versailles. Louis's sun symbol still appears on bottles of Chateldon, which is known in France as *la "Rolls" des eaux*—the Rolls-Royce of waters.

Chateldon,
FRANCE

CARBONATION natural TDS 1,882 mg/l HARDNESS 1,154 mg/l pH 6.2 NITRATE <1 mg/l CALCIUM 383 mg/l MAGNESIUM 49 mg/l SODIUM 240 mg/l POTASSIUM 35 mg/l BICARBONATE 2075 mg/l SULFATES 20 mg/l CHLORIDES 7 mg/l

VIRGINALITY: ◆ ◆ ◆ ◆ ◆
REGION: Auvergne
SOURCE: Spring
MINERALITY: Very High
HARDNESS: Very Hard
ORIENTATION: Acidic

CHAUD-FONTAINE

STILL | BOLD

ESTABLISHED 1924

Less known than the other major waters from Belgium (Spa and Bru) but with higher mineral content, Chaudfontaine has a neutral pH and a nice bicarbonate level. The low level of nitrate indicates an undisturbed source.

The thermal baths in Chaudfontaine have been used by humans since 1676. The 5,200-foot-deep (1,585 m) aquifer is well-covered by rock, which filters rainwater for about sixty years. When it reaches the surface, the spring water is a warm 99 degrees Fahrenheit (37°C).

Chaudfontaine,
BELGIUM

CARBONATION artificial TDS 385 mg/l HARDNESS 235 mg/l pH 7 NITRATE <1 mg/l CALCIUM 65 mg/l MAGNESIUM 18 mg/l SODIUM 44 mg/l POTASSIUM 3 mg/l BICARBONATE 305 mg/l SULFATES 40 mg/l CHLORIDES 35 mg/l

VIRGINALITY: ♦ ♦ ♦ ♦ ♦
REGION: Ardennes
SOURCE: Artesian
MINERALITY: Medium
HARDNESS: Very Hard
ORIENTATION: Neutral
VINTAGE: 60 years

CLOUD JUICE

ESTABLISHED 1993

STILL

Cloud Juice is a soft rainwater bottled at one of the most remote places in the world. It has a nice presentation and a story that is hard to beat. Tasmania, it seems, is becoming the rainwater capital of the world.

With the Cape Grim Weather Station nearby, King Island is home to some of the cleanest air in the world—and some of the cleanest rain. Duncan McFie had been harvesting this rain for personal use for some time when his friends started asking for bottles of his water. He set to work planning a system to harvest the water for commercial sales and built an expensive system including a roof, tank, and gutter. This original catchment had to be expanded as demand for Cloud Juice grew around the world.

King Island, AUSTRALIA

TDS NA HARDNESS 1 mg/l pH 7.3 NITRATE <1 mg/l CALCIUM 0.5 mg/l MAGNESIUM 0.05 mg/l SODIUM 10 mg/l POTASSIUM 1 mg/l SILICA NA BICARBONATE NA SULFATES 2 mg/l CHLORIDES 19 mg/l

VIRGINALITY: ♦ ♦ ♦ ♦ ♦

REGION: Tasmania

SOURCE: Rain

MINERALITY: Super Low

HARDNESS: Soft

ORIENTATION: Neutral

VINTAGE: I week

CONTREX

ESTABLISHED 1760

STILL

Contrex, with its high calcium content, has a sophisticated, acquired taste. The water is usually consumed as an everyday home drink—it's more a sports and fitness water than a beverage for epicurean use.

Water from precipitation surfaces at 51.8 degrees Fahrenheit (11°C) after filtering through limestone for two years. Nestlé, which recently began selling Contrex in the United States, highlights the water's diuretic value in its marketing—the water has a good reputation as a dieting aid. With 486 mg/l, Contrex's calcium content is extremely high; the water also features high levels of magnesium and sulfates but a surprisingly low amount of bicarbonate for a water with such high TDS.

Contrexéville,
FRANCE

TDS 2,125 mg/l HARDNESS 1,555 mg/l pH 7.3 NITRATE 2.7 mg/l CALCIUM 486 mg/l MAGNESIUM 84 mg/l SODIUM 9 mg/l POTASSIUM 3 mg/l BICARBONATE 403 mg/l SULFATES 1,187 mg/l CHLORIDES 10 mg/l

VIRGINALITY: ♦ ♦ ♦ ♦

REGION: Vosges

SOURCE: Spring at 870 feet (265 m)

MINERALITY: Very High

HARDNESS: Very Hard

ORIENTATION: Neutral

VINTAGE: 2 years

CRISTALINE
(ST. CECILE)

STILL

Cristaline St. Cecile comes from southern France and has a very favorable 1:2 ratio of magnesium to calcium. For a water with such a low TDS, Cristaline contains a significant level of bicarbonate.

One of France's bestselling brands, Cristaline-branded water actually comes from seventeen springs. Southern France has eight of them; others are scattered across the country. Each source offers a unique composition. Americans may be familiar with the St. Cecile version.

Val Chiusa-Cairanne,
FRANCE

TDS 270 mg/l **HARDNESS** 206 mg/l **pH** 7.6 **NITRATE** <1 mg/l
CALCIUM 44 mg/l **MAGNESIUM** 24 mg/l **SODIUM** 23 mg/l
POTASSIUM 2 mg/l **BICARBONATE** 287 mg/l **SULFATES** 3 mg/l
CHLORIDES 5 mg/l

VIRGINALITY: ♦ ♦ ♦ ♦ ♦
REGION: Provence-Alpes-Côte d'Azur
SOURCE: Spring
MINERALITY: Medium
HARDNESS: Very Hard
ORIENTATION: Hint of Sweet

DAGGIO

STILL | EFFERVESCENT

Daggio has a very low mineral content and a pH factor that lends a light, almost sweet perception. Its Effervescent artificial carbonation makes this water an excellent choice for mixed drinks.

High in the Orobic Alps, with a view of the Valsassina Valley in northern Italy, the source for Daggio is one of Europe's highest. The water, which emerges at 57.2 degrees Fahrenheit (14°C), is a good choice for infants and others who should avoid high TDS waters; the lightness of the water is another benefit. The Renaissance saw Daggio rise to fame; stocks of it were kept on hand by luminaries such as Leonardo da Vinci.

Daggio,
ITALY

CARBONATION artificial TDS 45 mg/l HARDNESS 4 mg/l pH 7.4 NITRATE 1.4 mg/l CALCIUM 8 mg/l MAGNESIUM 2 mg/l SODIUM 2 mg/l POTASSIUM 1 mg/l SILICA 7 mg/l BICARBONATE 41 mg/l SULFATES 5 mg/l CHLORIDES 1 mg/l

VIRGINALITY: ◆ ◆ ◆ ◆
REGION: Lombardia
SOURCE: Spring at 6,350 feet (1,935 m)
MINERALITY: Super Low
HARDNESS: Soft
ORIENTATION: Hint of Sweet

DIAMOND

Established 1968

STILL

You can enjoy this pristine, low mineral content water from a bottle or in frozen form. Diamond Ice comes as ten diamond-shaped ice cubes in a single-use plastic tray designed for those of us who care where our ice comes from. The ice is perfect for cocktails and the hospitality industry.

Very clean air and water can be found in Tasmania, some of the nearest hospitable land to Antarctica. Wind between 40 and 50 degrees latitude—known by sailors as the "Roaring Forties"—sweeps over the ocean and brings rain into the highlands of Tasmania, where springs formed thousands of years ago. Water for Diamond and Diamond Ice is taken from one of these springs, which is located amid caves and rainforest.

Great Western Tiers,
Australia

TDS 234 mg/l HARDNESS 100 mg/l pH 4.7 NITRATE <1 mg/l CALCIUM 35 mg/l MAGNESIUM 3 mg/l SODIUM 39 mg/l POTASSIUM 0.5 mg/l BICARBONATE 237 mg/l SULFATES 4 mg/l CHLORIDES 35 mg/l

VIRGINALITY: ◆◆◆◆◆
REGION: Tasmania
SOURCE: Spring
MINERALITY: Low
HARDNESS: Moderately Hard
ORIENTATION: Acidic

DONAT MG

Established 1967

LIGHT

*Donat Mg (Mg for "magnesium")
has one of the highest mineral con-
tents of any bottled water in the
world. With a TDS of a whopping
13,298 mg/l, it's in a class of its
own. The mineral taste is very
distinct, and the water feels very
substantial on the palate. It can
be served as a digestivo and is
best consumed in small doses.*

In 1572 the foundation stone
was laid for a spa in Rogaška
Slatina; the first chemical analysis of the waters was carried out
in the next century. The spa and
its healthful waters remain a
draw. The extremely high level of
magnesium in Donat Mg—more
than 1,000 mg/l—make it especially desirable, and it is thought to
have strong curative powers. The
spring reaches as deep as 2,000 feet
(610 m).

Donat,
Slovenia

CARBONATION natural TDS 13,298 mg/l HARDNESS
5,315 mg/l pH 6.8 NITRATE <1 mg/l CALCIUM 420 mg/l
MAGNESIUM 1,060 mg/l SODIUM 1,600 mg/l POTASSIUM
17 mg/l BICARBONATE 7,700 mg/l SULFATES 2,250 mg/l
CHLORIDES 74 mg/l

VIRGINALITY: ♦ ♦ ♦ ♦ ♦

REGION: Rogaška Slatina

SOURCE: Well

MINERALITY: Very High

HARDNESS: Very Hard

ORIENTATION: Neutral

DUCALE

STILL   EFFERVESCENT

Another classic Italian Alpine, low mineral content water with an Effervescent carbonation. Green glass bottles with crown caps make for a nice presentation (though the company also uses clear glass, as shown here). Ducale is a good alternative to sparkling waters with high mineral content and low carbonation.

A protected aquifer with no pollution is the source of Ducale, which emerges from the spring at 48.2 degrees Fahrenheit (9°C). More than a thousand years ago, monks used Ducale as holy water.

Monte Zuccone,
ITALY

CARBONATION 2.4 mg/l artificial **TDS** 55 mg/l **HARDNESS** 65 mg/l **pH** 7.8 **NITRATE** 1.9 mg/l **CALCIUM** 13 mg/l **MAGNESIUM** 1 mg/l **SODIUM** 3 mg/l **POTASSIUM** <1 mg/l **SILICA** 5 mg/l **BICARBONATE** 40 mg/l **SULFATES** 7 mg/l **CHLORIDES** 4 mg/l

VIRGINALITY: ♦ ♦ ♦ ♦
REGION: Parma Apennines
SOURCE: Spring at 3,116 feet (950 m)
MINERALITY: Low
HARDNESS: Moderately Hard
ORIENTATION: Alkaline

EAUZONE

Established 2005

STILL   LIGHT   CLASSIC

A low TDS water with a nice pH, Eauzone comes from a pristine source and is available in sparkling and light sparkling versions. To teach children the importance of drinking water instead of sodas and other sugary drinks, Eauzone developed the Lara and Luna characters for their cute children's collection.

The source was hidden in the forest of Glencar Valley until 2003. Swaths of limestone form hills in the mountains around Glencar Lake. While the valleys are mostly made up of shale, glacial deposits of sand and gravel can also be found there. This geology filters the water for about a century, imparting only a low level of mineral content.

Glencar Valley,
Ireland

CARBONATION artificial TDS 167 mg/l HARDNESS 136 mg/l
pH 7.3 NITRATE <1 mg/l CALCIUM 35 mg/l MAGNESIUM
12 mg/l SODIUM 10 mg/l POTASSIUM 5 mg/l SILICA 2 mg/l
BICARBONATE 167 mg/l SULFATES 50 mg/l CHLORIDES
12 mg/l

VIRGINALITY: ♦ ♦ ♦ ♦ ♦
REGION: County Sligo
SOURCE: Spring
MINERALITY: Low
HARDNESS: Hard
ORIENTATION: Neutral
VINTAGE: 100 years

ELDORADO

ESTABLISHED 1983

STILL

Eldorado is an award-winning, low mineral content water with a possible sweet perception and a very neutral overall taste. In blind water tastings, Eldorado stands out.

An aquifer 8,000 feet (2,438 m) below ground at Eldorado Canyon absorbs water from rain and snow near the Continental Divide. The water surfaces at 76 degrees Fahrenheit (24°C) in Eldorado Springs, forced through the sandstone by artesian pressure. Five hundred feet (152 m) of clay covering the sandstone protect the water from contamination, and vast parkland surrounding the area protects the springs from development.

Eldorado Springs, USA

TDS 82 mg/l **HARDNESS** 35 mg/l **pH** 7.3 **NITRATE** <1 mg/l **CALCIUM** 14 mg/l **MAGNESIUM** 4 mg/l **SODIUM** 7 mg/l **POTASSIUM** 3 mg/l **BICARBONATE** 0 mg/l **SULFATES** 21 mg/l **CHLORIDES** 2 mg/l

VIRGINALITY: ♦ ♦ ♦ ♦ ♦

REGION: Colorado

SOURCE: Artesian

MINERALITY: Low

HARDNESS: Slightly Hard

ORIENTATION: Neutral

ENGLISH MOUNTAIN

ESTABLISHED 1997

A superior source produces this low mineral content water, with a pH that gives a sweet perception. English Mountain is sold under its own brand and in many custom-label bottlings.

Each day 2.5 million gallons (9.5 million l) of water flow at 58 degrees Fahrenheit (14°C) from the spring in the Great Smoky Mountains. During Prohibition, a drink of the water may have chased a glass of moonshine served at the dance hall that shared the name of the spring: Promised Land. The Berkley Springs water-tasting competition named English Mountain the best noncarbonated water in 1999.

Chestnut Hill,
Dandridge, USA

TDS 140 mg/l **HARDNESS** 27 mg/l **pH** 7.66 **NITRATE** 0.38 mg/l **CALCIUM** NA **MAGNESIUM** 6.8 mg/l **SODIUM** 1.5 mg/l **POTASSIUM** 1.2 mg/l **BICARBONATE** 100 mg/l **SULFATES** 8.3 mg/l **CHLORIDES** 1.2 mg/l

VIRGINALITY: ♦ ♦ ♦ ♦ ♦

REGION: Tennessee

SOURCE: Spring at 2,100 feet (640 m)

MINERALITY: Low

HARDNESS: Slightly Hard

ORIENTATION: Hint of Sweet

EVIAN

ESTABLISHED 1826

STILL

A megabrand associated with health, youth, beauty, fitness, and celebrity, Evian is the standard for still water in many trendy restaurants.

The Marquis de Lessert discovered the Alpine source of Evian water in 1789. Before the water—which originates in the French Alps as rain and snow—reaches the source on Lake Geneva's southern shore, it is filtered by a subterranean aquifer for fifteen years or more, picking up minerals from the glacial sand to give the water its distinctive taste. Evian today is one of the world's most recognizable brands of bottled water; the company's product range also includes a beauty and healthcare line.

Evian-les-Bains,
FRANCE

TDS 357 mg/l HARDNESS 291 mg/l pH 7.2 NITRATE 3.8 mg/l CALCIUM 78 mg/l MAGNESIUM 24 mg/l SODIUM 5 mg/l POTASSIUM 1 mg/l SILICA 14 mg/l BICARBONATE 357 mg/l SULFATES 10 mg/l CHLORIDES 5 mg/l

VIRGINALITY: ◆ ◆ ◆ ◆

REGION: Haute Savoie

SOURCE: Spring at 2,500 feet (762 m)

MINERALITY: Medium

HARDNESS: Very Hard

ORIENTATION: Neutral

VINTAGE: 15 years

FAMOUS CRAZY WATER

Established 1914

STILL

The water is available as Deep Well, a high mineral content water, and Drinking Water, with all mineral content removed. The two are meant to be mixed together to achieve a custom mineral level. High in sodium (giving it a salty perception) and bicarbonate, Famous Crazy Water is a meal in itself.

Mineral Wells, Texas, boomed when mineral water was discovered there in 1880. The subsequent decades saw a number of wells dug, and droves of people came to enjoy the water's health benefits. The Famous Mineral Water Company's well is still in use today.

Mineral Wells, USA

TDS 2,763 mg/l **HARDNESS** 156 mg/l **pH** 7.6 **NITRATE** <1 mg/l **CALCIUM** 32 mg/l **MAGNESIUM** 19 mg/l **SODIUM** 904 mg/l **POTASSIUM** 5 mg/l **BICARBONATE** 758 mg/l **SULFATES** 1,170 mg/l **CHLORIDES** 200 mg/l

VIRGINALITY: ♦ ♦ ♦ ♦ ♦
REGION: Texas
SOURCE: Well
MINERALITY: Very High
HARDNESS: Hard
ORIENTATION: Hint of Sweet

FERRARELLE

Ferrarelle is one of the very few naturally carbonated mineral waters. The high level of bicarbonate assists digestion, and the soft, small bubbles give the water some pleasing structure. Ferrarelle is also a significant source of calcium.

The spring, which is inland from Naples, has been known since before the Romans; Hannibal, it is said, stopped at the spring with his troops. The water surfaces at 59 degrees Fahrenheit (15°C) and is naturally carbonated by carbon dioxide pockets created by Mount Vesuvius, an active volcano 40 miles (64 km) from the spring. One of Italy's most popular sparkling waters, Ferrarelle is commonly seen accompanying food in Rome, Florence, and Naples, though the water is not well-known in the United States.

Ferrarelle, Val D'Assano, ITALY

CARBONATION 2.1 mg/l natural TDS 1,270 mg/l HARDNESS 577 mg/l pH 6.1 NITRATE 5 mg/l CALCIUM 362 mg/l MAGNESIUM 18 mg/l SODIUM 49 mg/l POTASSIUM 43 mg/l SILICA 81 mg/l BICARBONATE 1,372 mg/l SULFATES 6 mg/l CHLORIDES 21 mg/l

VIRGINALITY: ◆ ◆ ◆
REGION: Naples
SOURCE: Spring at 1,500 feet (457 m)
MINERALITY: High
HARDNESS: Very Hard
ORIENTATION: Acidic

FIJI

Established 1996

A low mineral content water, high in silica, with a possible sweet perception and an overall smooth sensation.

Before it reaches the aquifer on Viti Levu, Fiji water begins as rain falling on the island's highlands and tropical forests. Volcanic rock filters the rainwater, and the remoteness of the island ensures that it is uncontaminated by artificial substances. The water was first sold in the United States in 1997; its great success can be attributed to a celebrity-oriented marketing campaign and the appealing bottle.

Yaqara Valley,
Fiji

TDS 210 mg/l **HARDNESS** 95 mg/l **pH** 7.5 **NITRATE** 0.26 mg/l **CALCIUM** 17 mg/l **MAGNESIUM** 13 mg/l **SODIUM** 17 mg/l **POTASSIUM** 5 mg/l **SILICA** 85 mg/l **BICARBONATE** 140 mg/l **SULFATES** NA **CHLORIDES** 9 mg/l

VIRGINALITY: ♦ ♦ ♦ ♦ ♦
REGION: Viti Levu
SOURCE: Artesian at 4,000 feet (1,220 m)
MINERALITY: Low
HARDNESS: Moderately Hard
ORIENTATION: Hint of Sweet
VINTAGE: 450 years

FINÉ

Established 1989

STILL

A stunning presentation, Finé's bottle is modeled after traditional sake bottles. It is contemporary but not out of place in an epicurean setting. Finé is a slightly hard, low mineral content water with a possible sweet and soft perception due to the pH factor and the amount of silica. I love Finé with caviar, for both taste and presentation.

Open a bottle of Finé today, and you will drink water formed more than a thousand years ago, before the water could encounter artificial contaminants. Rainwater takes on a unique mineral composition while filtering through thick volcanic rock on the way to the aquifer 2,100 feet (600 m) below the Fuji volcanic base.

Shuzenji,
JAPAN

TDS 140 mg/l **HARDNESS** 45 mg/l **pH** 7.8 **NITRATE** <1 mg/l
CALCIUM 14 mg/l **MAGNESIUM** 5 mg/l **SODIUM** 9 mg/l
POTASSIUM 2 mg/l **SILICA** 82 mg/l **BICARBONATE** 62 mg/l
SULFATES 10 mg/l **CHLORIDES** 5 mg/l

VIRGINALITY: ♦ ♦ ♦ ♦ ♦

REGION: Izu Peninsula

SOURCE: Artesian

MINERALITY: Low

HARDNESS: Slightly Hard

ORIENTATION: Alkaline

VINTAGE: 1,000 years

FIUGGI

STILL

BOLD

A curative with a low mineral content, fairly significant carbonation, and an almost neutral pH factor, Fiuggi is at home in an epicurean setting. It is water that draws attention. The unique composition also makes it perfect for mixed drinks. It has an impressive presentation; I especially like the blue bottle for the sparkling version.

Since the Middle Ages, people have visited the spa at Fiuggi, about 40 miles (64 km) south of Rome, for its curative water with diuretic properties. Even today, the water is prescribed to combat and prevent kidney stones. Fiuggi, which emerges from its spring at 51.8 degrees Fahrenheit (11°C), has always been popular in the Vatican, and in 1548 even the artist Michelangelo wrote of having experienced its benefits.

Fiuggi,
ITALY

CARBONATION 8 mg/l artificial TDS 122 mg/l HARDNESS 60 mg/l pH 6.8 NITRATE 7 mg/l CALCIUM 16 mg/l MAGNESIUM 6 mg/l SODIUM 6 mg/l POTASSIUM 4 mg/l SILICA 13 mg/l BICARBONATE 82 mg/l SULFATES 6 mg/l CHLORIDES 14 mg/l

VIRGINALITY: ◆ ◆ ◆
REGION: Rome
SOURCE: Spring
MINERALITY: Low
HARDNESS: Slightly Hard
ORIENTATION: Neutral

FONT SELVA

STILL

A low mineral content water from the Girona region of Spain with elevated bicarbonate levels, which should be beneficial for digestion.

The ancients recognized the quality of the water from Girona's La Selva region, which features large, unique formations of granite. The spring lies in a high, lush valley of Les Guilleries mountains, 4.5 miles (7 km) from Sant Hilari Sacalm, "the town of the one hundred springs."

Sant Hilari Sacalm,
SPAIN

TDS 229 mg/l **HARDNESS** 80 mg/l **pH** 7.6 **NITRATE** <1 mg/l
CALCIUM 34 mg/l **MAGNESIUM** 5 mg/l **SODIUM** 50 mg/l
POTASSIUM 7 mg/l **SILICA** 23 mg/l **BICARBONATE** 216 mg/l
SULFATES 11 mg/l **CHLORIDES** 12 mg/l

VIRGINALITY: ◆ ◆ ◆ ◆ ◆
REGION: Girona
SOURCE: Spring
MINERALITY: Low
HARDNESS: Moderately Hard
ORIENTATION: Hint of Sweet
VINTAGE: 20 years

GALVANINA

Established 1901

STILL   CLASSIC

The medium TDS, neutral pH, and choice of Still or sparkling versions make this water a classic—especially since it is available in glass. A perfect match for almost any food.

Well-known Roman baths were built near the spring. Huge clay banks from the Pliocene epoch cover the dense quartz sand that filters the water before it slowly flows under the Apennines to the hill where it surfaces, San Lorenzo Monte. First bottled in 1901, Galvanina is showcased in a series of traditional glass bottles.

Galvanina,
Italy

CARBONATION 6.5 mg/l artificial **TDS** 475 mg/l **HARDNESS** 362 mg/l **pH** 7.1 **NITRATE** <1 mg/l **CALCIUM** 113 mg/l **MAGNESIUM** 20 mg/l **SODIUM** 33 mg/l **POTASSIUM** 1 mg/l **SILICA** 6 mg/l **BICARBONATE** 365 mg/l **SULFATES** 89 mg/l **CHLORIDES** 33 mg/l

VIRGINALITY: ♦ ♦ ♦ ♦ ♦
REGION: Rimini
SOURCE: Spring
MINERALITY: Medium
HARDNESS: Very Hard
ORIENTATION: Neutral

GEROLSTEINER

ESTABLISHED 1888

STILL   LIGHT   CLASSIC

Drinking this water is like taking mineral supplements. A high TDS means Gerolsteiner, much like Apollinaris, is best enjoyed pure rather than in a mixed drink.

Archaeological evidence dates knowledge of the water to Roman times and even prehistory. Volcanic activity near the aquifer naturally carbonates the water to about 3.5 mg/l. The carbon dioxide damages the twenty or so artesian wells from which the water is sourced, so new wells are drilled every twenty years. To produce the Light "Stille Quelle" water with 4 mg/l of carbonation and the Classic "Sprudel" with 8 mg/l, additional carbon dioxide is extracted from the source used by the water itself and added during bottling. The water surfaces at 52 degrees Fahrenheit (11°C).

Gerolstein,
GERMANY

CARBONATION 4 mg/l, 8 mg/l natural **TDS** 2,527 mg/l
HARDNESS 1,299 mg/l **pH** 5.9 NITRATE 5.1 mg/l CALCIUM
347 mg/l **MAGNESIUM** 108 mg/l SODIUM 119 mg/l
POTASSIUM 11 mg/l **SILICA** 40 mg/l BICARBONATE
1,817 mg/l SULFATES 36 mg/l CHLORIDES 40 mg/l

VIRGINALITY: ◆ ◆ ◆
REGION: Rheinland-Pfalz
SOURCE: Artesian
MINERALITY: Very High
HARDNESS: Very Hard
ORIENTATION: Acidic

GLENEAGLES

ESTABLISHED 1995

STILL   LIGHT

An attention-grabbing bottle makes this Still and Effervescent water highly presentable. The water has a low TDS and an alkaline pH. Try it with dishes that might be overpowered by a high mineral content but still call for a little bit of structure. Unfortunately, the water has an elevated nitrate level.

The water spends fifteen years trickling through the rocks of the Ochil Hills and absorbing minerals there before being bottled at the famous Scottish estate of Gleneagles. The attractive bottle is an award winner. In 2001 Gleneagles was acquired by the nearby bottler of Highland Spring.

Blackford,
UNITED KINGDOM

CARBONATION artificial TDS 235 mg/l HARDNESS 143 mg/l
pH 8 NITRATE 8 mg/l CALCIUM 46 mg/l MAGNESIUM 7 mg/l
SODIUM 12 mg/l POTASSIUM 1 mg/l BICARBONATE 136 mg/l
SULFATES 11 mg/l CHLORIDES 43 mg/l

VIRGINALITY: ♦ ♦
REGION: Scotland
SOURCE: Spring
MINERALITY: Low
HARDNESS: Very Hard
ORIENTATION: Alkaline
VINTAGE: 15 years

GOCCIA DI CARNIA

STILL   EFFERVESCENT

This is a very light water with minimal sodium content (virtually sodium free). It can have diuretic effects and is recommended for low-sodium diets. The water is available in glass and plastic and is perfect for dishes that require a low minerality water.

The source 4,495 feet (1,370 m) up the Carnian Alps is replenished by snow that melts after each winter. Larch forest surrounds the source, which brings water to the surface at 43 degrees Fahrenheit (6°C). Water is bottled at the source.

Forni Avoltri,
ITALY

CARBONATION 1.5 mg/l artificial TDS 69 mg/l HARDNESS 60 mg/l pH 8.34 NITRATE 1.6 mg/l CALCIUM 18 mg/l MAGNESIUM 4 mg/l SODIUM 1.2 mg/l POTASSIUM 1 mg/l BICARBONATE 79 mg/l SULFATES 2.8 mg/l CHLORIDES 1 mg/l

VIRGINALITY: ♦ ♦ ♦

REGION: Udine, Friuli-Venezia Giulia

SOURCE: Spring

MINERALITY: Low

HARDNESS: Slightly Hard

ORIENTATION: Alkaline

HADHAM

ESTABLISHED 1990

STILL | CLASSIC

This medium TDS water is high in calcium and low in sodium. Hadham is available in classic, understated glass; unfortunately, a very high nitrate level prevents the water's quality from matching that of the bottle's design.

A 500-foot (152 m) stretch of chalk in the Ash Valley purifies Hadham water, which was first bottled by the family-owned company in 1990. The water may be purchased in either glass or plastic bottles.

Little Hadham,
UNITED KINGDOM

CARBONATION artificial TDS 400 mg/l HARDNESS 300 mg/l
pH 7.4 NITRATE 25 mg/l CALCIUM 115 mg/l MAGNESIUM
3 mg/l SODIUM 7 mg/l POTASSIUM 2 mg/l SILICA 21 mg/l
BICARBONATE 252 mg/l SULFATES 12 mg/l CHLORIDES
10 mg/l

VIRGINALITY: ♦

REGION: Hertfordshire

SOURCE: Spring

MINERALITY: Medium

HARDNESS: Very Hard

ORIENTATION: Hint of Sweet

HARGHITA

EFFERVESCENT

Harghita is a medium TDS water with a fairly even taste, which made it famous in Europe. It's a nice alternative to the heavier Borsec and contains enough bicarbonate to benefit digestion. Harghita is widely considered to be a curative.

The free-flowing spring is located 1,000 feet (305 m) above sea level in the picturesque Harghita Mountains. Industry is not found near the region, which is protected by the Romanian government.

Braşov,
ROMANIA

CARBONATION 2.5 mg/l natural TDS 770 mg/l HARDNESS 559 mg/l pH 6.2 NITRATE NA CALCIUM 113 mg/l MAGNESIUM 69 mg/l SODIUM 68 mg/l POTASSIUM 11 mg/l BICARBONATE 854 mg/l SULFATES <1 mg/l CHLORIDES 2 mg/l

VIRGINALITY: Not Available

REGION: Carpathian Alps

SOURCE: Spring at 1,000 feet (305 m)

MINERALITY: Medium

HARDNESS: Very Hard

ORIENTATION: Acidic

HARROGATE SPA

Established 2002

STILL   CLASSIC

The low mineral content and nice glass bottle fit well in any epicurean setting. The water is very low in sodium and high in bicarbonate. The low nitrate level indicates an unspoiled source.

A unique geological formation—the Harrogate Anticline and Fault—carries rainwater vertically into Harlow Hill and deeper within the earth to an aquifer of sandstone between layers of mudstone. Only several hundred years later do fault lines carry the water to Harrogate's many springs. Stronger mineral waters are found lower on the hill, where the water has had more chance to dissolve minerals. The well for bottling is located at the top of the hill, where the water has a lower TDS.

Harrogate,
United Kingdom

CARBONATION 6 mg/l artificial **TDS** 225 mg/l **HARDNESS** 197 mg/l **pH** 6.7 **NITRATE** <1 mg/l **CALCIUM** 53 mg/l **MAGNESIUM** 16 mg/l **SODIUM** 6 mg/l **POTASSIUM** 3 mg/l **BICARBONATE** 235 mg/l **SULFATES** 7 mg/l **CHLORIDES** 21 mg/l

VIRGINALITY: ♦ ♦ ♦ ♦ ♦
REGION: North Yorkshire
SOURCE: Spring
MINERALITY: Low
HARDNESS: Very Hard
ORIENTATION: Neutral
VINTAGE: 300 years

HAWAIIAN SPRINGS

STILL

An interesting young water with very low mineral content. This is as close to Hawaiian rain as it gets—try using the water to make ice cubes for tropical drinks.

On average, 143 inches (363 cm) of rain fall each year at Kea'au, which means "clear, pure spring water." The area has no streams to sweep this water away, so it seeps into the volcanic rock of Mauna Loa and Kilauea, spending only about thirty days there before reaching the aquifer. As a result, the water remains young and low in minerals; it is bottled daily.

Kea'au, District of
Puna, USA

TDS 64 mg/l HARDNESS 34 mg/l pH 7.7 NITRATE <1 mg/l
CALCIUM 7 mg/l MAGNESIUM 3 mg/l SODIUM 6 mg/l
POTASSIUM 2 mg/l SILICA NA BICARBONATE 34 mg/l
SULFATES 5 mg/l CHLORIDES 4 mg/l

VIRGINALITY: ♦ ♦ ♦ ♦ ♦
REGION: Big Island, Hawaii
SOURCE: Artesian
MINERALITY: Low
HARDNESS: Slightly Hard
ORIENTATION: Hint of Sweet
VINTAGE: 30 days

HIGHLAND SPRING

ESTABLISHED 1979

STILL   LIGHT

The fine, small bubbles make this low mineral content water a favorite of many. Highland Spring is perfect with your scotch and is also a good water for making ice cubes. The glass bottles would benefit from a design update (plastic bottles are also used, as shown here).

Rain falling on the beautiful, ancient Ochil Hills in Perthshire is filtered for fifteen years by 400-million-year-old layers of red sandstone and basalt. Cavities in the rock lend minerals to the water before it is extracted through 197-foot (60 m) stainless steel pipes sunk in boreholes, each of which pumps as much as 2,900 gallons (11,000 l) per hour. The water is untouched before bottling, save for filtration of sand and grit.

Blackford,
UNITED KINGDOM

CARBONATION artificial TDS 136 mg/l HARDNESS 124 mg/l pH 7.8 NITRATE <1 mg/l CALCIUM 35 mg/l MAGNESIUM 9 mg/l SODIUM 6 mg/l POTASSIUM 1 mg/l BICARBONATE 136 mg/l SULFATES 6 mg/l CHLORIDES 8 mg/l

VIRGINALITY: ♦ ♦ ♦ ♦ ♦
REGION: Scotland
SOURCE: Well at 1,398 feet (426 m)
MINERALITY: Low
HARDNESS: Hard
ORIENTATION: Alkaline
VINTAGE: 15 years

HILDON

ESTABLISHED 1989

STILL   LIGHT

*I love finding Hildon's understated
bottle in an epicurean context.
The Still version is labeled
"Delightfully Still," and the very
effervescent sparkling version is
"Gently Carbonated."*

The owners of the Hildon were
aware of the estate's water source
when they acquired the site in the
mid-1980s. They soon tested the
water and submitted it to
European authorities to be legally
recognized as natural mineral
water. In the early part of the following decade, the London hospitality industry contributed to
strong growth of the water, which
is not treated during bottling. Sales
in 2005 reached more than two
million cases—about ten percent of
those cases were exported.

Hildon Estate,
UNITED KINGDOM

CARBONATION 2.8 mg/l artificial TDS 312 mg/l HARDNESS
250 mg/l pH 7.2 NITRATE 5.6 mg/l CALCIUM 97 mg/l
MAGNESIUM 2 mg/l SODIUM 8 mg/l POTASSIUM NA SILICA
NA BICARBONATE 136 mg/l SULFATES 4 mg/l CHLORIDES
16 mg/l

VIRGINALITY: ◆ ◆ ◆
REGION: Hampshire
SOURCE: Well
MINERALITY: Medium
HARDNESS: Very Hard
ORIENTATION: Neutral

ICE AGE

ESTABLISHED 1995

STILL

An extremely low mineral content characterizes this very soft water, which is close to rainwater in its characteristics. Ice Age can best be described as distilled water with terroir.

The source's terrain is too steep to support human or animal life, so the water remains very pure when it falls to the granite pools at the base of the source. Water is harvested from these pools (just before the point at which it would join the ocean) and taken to a bottling facility 250 miles (400 km) away in Vancouver—environmental restrictions prevent industrial activity on the glacier.

NOTE: Do not confuse this water with the Glacier Water vending machines found outside grocery stores. These machines dispense filtered local tap water.

Toba Inlet,
CANADA

TDS 4 mg/l HARDNESS 1 mg/l pH 5.5 NITRATE 0.1 mg/l
CALCIUM 0.4 mg/l MAGNESIUM 0.1 mg/l SODIUM 0 mg/l
POTASSIUM 0 mg/l BICARBONATE 0 mg/l SULFATES 0.5 mg/l
CHLORIDES 0 mg/l

VIRGINALITY: ♦ ♦ ♦ ♦ ♦
REGION: British Columbia
SOURCE: Glacier
MINERALITY: Super Low
HARDNESS: Soft
ORIENTATION: Acidic

ICELANDIC GLACIAL

Established 2003

This very low mineral content water is sourced from an extremely remote area of our planet. The award-winning square bottle comes with four different labels, which form an icy landscape if put side by side.

A volcano erupting 4,500 years ago formed the Ölfus spring; lava rock from this eruption protects the aquifer from external contamination. A stainless steel pipe carries water from the spring to the bottling plant. Agriculture and construction is prohibited by the local government in the 128,000-acre (51,800 hectares) exclusion zone surrounding the spring.

Thorlákshöfn,
Iceland

TDS 68 mg/l **HARDNESS** 26 mg/l **pH** 7.75 **NITRATE** <1 mg/l **CALCIUM** 6 mg/l **MAGNESIUM** 2 mg/l **SODIUM** 12 mg/l **POTASSIUM** 1 mg/l **BICARBONATE** NA **SULFATES** 3 mg/l **CHLORIDES** 13 mg/l

VIRGINALITY: ♦ ♦ ♦ ♦ ♦
REGION: Ölfus
SOURCE: Spring
MINERALITY: Low
HARDNESS: Slightly Hard
ORIENTATION: Hint of Sweet

ICELAND SPRING

Established 1990

STILL

Iceland Spring has very low mineral content and a high alkaline pH, which lends a hint of bitterness to the taste. The water is low in sodium and essentially nitrate free, indicating a pristine source.

Water from rain and snow falling in the mountains outside Reykjavík picks up a small amount of minerals as it travels through volcanic rock on its way to a subterranean river that supplies the spring. Though the natural spring is located in the Heidmörk nature reserve, on a 150-acre (61 hectares) site inaccessible to animals as well as unauthorized humans, the water for bottling is actually piped from a borehole drilled at a higher elevation.

Heidmörk,
Iceland

TDS 48 mg/l **HARDNESS** 25 mg/l **pH** 8.7 **NITRATE** 0.06 mg/l
CALCIUM 5 mg/l **MAGNESIUM** 1 mg/l **SODIUM** 12 mg/l
POTASSIUM 0 mg/l **SILICA** 14 mg/l **BICARBONATE** 27 mg/l
SULFATES 2 mg/l **CHLORIDES** 10 mg/l

VIRGINALITY: ♦ ♦ ♦ ♦ ♦
REGION: Reykjavík
SOURCE: Spring
MINERALITY: Super Low
HARDNESS: Slightly Hard
ORIENTATION: Alkaline

KAISER WASSER

ESTABLISHED 1968

FINEWATERS BALANCE

 STILL   BOLD

Kaiser Wasser has a distinguished history of use as a curative throughout Europe. The medium mineral content water has a nice pH and good levels of calcium and bicarbonate. The presentation reminds me of an era long gone, when emperors ruled this part of Europe.

Ancient Illyrian pottery has been found near the spring, which was thought to provide healthful waters in both the pre-Roman and Roman periods. Continuous curative use of the waters has occurred from the time of Benedictine control of the thermal baths, from 769 through 1500. Central European high society flocked to the Grand Thermal Hotel Wildbad in the middle of the nineteenth century. Water surfaces at 43 degrees Fahrenheit (6°C).

San Candido,
ITALY

CARBONATION 14 mg/l artificial TDS 770 mg/l HARDNESS 614 mg/l pH 7.52 NITRATE 1.1 mg/l CALCIUM 180 mg/l MAGNESIUM 41 mg/l SODIUM 1 mg/l POTASSIUM <1 mg/l SILICA 6 mg/l BICARBONATE 230 mg/l SULFATES 400 mg/l CHLORIDES <1 mg/l

VIRGINALITY: ◆ ◆ ◆ ◆
REGION: South Tyrol
SOURCE: Spring at 3,970 feet (1,210 m)
MINERALITY: Medium
HARDNESS: Very Hard
ORIENTATION: Hint of Sweet

KAROO

STILL | LIGHT

This award-winning South African water comes in a stunning glass bottle. The medium mineral content water from a pristine source has a very favorable pH and low nitrate levels.

Karoo comes from a source on the Paardeberg granite massif, part of the Malmesbury Group and the Cape Granite Suite. The bottling company dug out and bricked in the area surrounding the spring to protect it from the elements. The water reaches the bottling facility through a pipeline. There is neither habitation nor agriculture in the mountain veld from which the spring absorbs rainwater. About 500 gallons (1,900 l) of water flow through the spring every hour.

Weltevrede Estate,
SOUTH AFRICA

CARBONATION 3 mg/l artificial TDS 378 mg/l HARDNESS 145 mg/l pH 7.50 NITRATE <1 mg/l CALCIUM 47 mg/l MAGNESIUM 7 mg/l SODIUM 22 mg/l POTASSIUM 2 mg/l BICARBONATE 80 mg/l SULFATES 10 mg/l CHLORIDES 50 mg/l

VIRGINALITY: ♦ ♦ ♦ ♦ ♦
REGION: Paarl
SOURCE: Spring
MINERALITY: Medium
HARDNESS: Hard
ORIENTATION: Hint of Sweet

KONA DEEP

ESTABLISHED 2005

STILL

This three-thousand-year-old desalinated deep sea water has a great story. Bottled water connoisseurs will be interested in this water as a curiosity.

Changes to the climate in the North Atlantic thousands of years ago melted icebergs off the coast of Greenland; while remaining distinct from the ocean water it displaced, the cold water that was produced sank rapidly to the ocean floor. Global currents now circulate this water, which is brought to the surface by the Natural Energy Laboratory of Hawaii's 3,000-foot (914 m) pipeline and bottled as Kona Deep. An advanced, double-pass, reverse osmosis process desalinizes the water before it is bottled.

Kona,
USA

TDS 224 mg/l **HARDNESS** 13 mg/l **pH** 6.5 **NITRATE** <1 mg/l **CALCIUM** 1 mg/l **MAGNESIUM** 2.5 mg/l **SODIUM** 76 mg/l **POTASSIUM** 4 mg/l **SILICA** 1 mg/l **SULFATES** 4 mg/l **CHLORIDES** 135 mg/l

VIRGINALITY: ◆ ◆ ◆ ◆ ◆

REGION: Big Island, Hawaii

SOURCE: Deep Sea at 3,000 feet (914 m)

MINERALITY: Low

HARDNESS: Soft

ORIENTATION: Acidic

VINTAGE: 3,000 years

L'AUBADE

ESTABLISHED 1995

STILL   EFFERVESCENT

This low mineral content water from South Africa is very soft, with a slightly acidic pH and extremely low nitrate levels. The stunning PET presentation is a very contemporary interpretation of a traditional bottle.

Franschhoek, where the Franschhoek Water Company bottles L'Aubade, is known as the "Gourmet Capital" of South Africa. The source in the Mont Rochelle Nature Reserve is free of human habitation and agriculture. The reserve's Middagkransberg Mountains contain layers of quartzitic sandstone, which filter rainwater that will eventually emerge at 62 degrees Fahrenheit (17°C). No further treatment is given to the water except filtration of fine particles and exposure to ultraviolet light.

L'Aubade Estate,
SOUTH AFRICA

CARBONATION 2.4 mg/l artificial TDS 61 mg/l HARDNESS 10 mg/l pH 6 NITRATE <1 mg/l CALCIUM 1 mg/l MAGNESIUM 2 mg/l SODIUM 12 mg/l POTASSIUM 1 mg/l SILICA 5 mg/l SULFATES 3 mg/l CHLORIDES 21 mg/l

VIRGINALITY: ♦ ♦ ♦ ♦ ♦
REGION: Franschhoek
SOURCE: Spring
MINERALITY: Low
HARDNESS: Soft
ORIENTATION: Acidic

LAUQUEN

Established 2005

STILL   CLASSIC

Lauquen is a high-style product for the global luxury market. It has low mineral content and comes from one of the most remote regions in the world.

Lauquen begins as ice and rain in the Andes. This artesian water surfaces at 39 degrees Fahrenheit (4°C) with unique mineral content after traveling up 1,500 feet (457 m) from the aquifer under its own pressure. The water emerges in a hollow in San Carlos Bariloche, Patagonia, where it is bottled at the source before exposure to air spoils the quality.

San Carlos de Bariloche, ARGENTINA

CARBONATION 6 mg/l artificial **TDS** 190 mg/l **HARDNESS** 80 mg/l **pH** 7.2 **NITRATE** 1 mg/l **CALCIUM** 22 mg/l **MAGNESIUM** 2 mg/l **SODIUM** 4 mg/l **BICARBONATE** 48 mg/l **SULFATES** 95 mg/l **CHLORIDES** NA

VIRGINALITY: ♦ ♦ ♦ ♦ ♦

REGION: Patagonia

SOURCE: Artesian

MINERALITY: Low

HARDNESS: Medium Hard

ORIENTATION: Neutral

LAURETANA

ESTABLISHED 1964

STILL   BOLD

One of the lightest naturally bottled waters in the world, the truly delightful Lauretana is bottled without filtering or processing. The water is available in a glass bottle designed by the Italian company Pininfarina.

Though the nearby Graglia Bagni spa was founded in 1883 in the Aosta Valley—where the air quality was famed and springs were abundant—the Lauretana spring was known by the ancients. Winter snow on the unpopulated slopes of Mombarone feeds the spring, but the flow is highest during the spring. Gravity carries water through stainless steel pipes to the plant farther down the mountainside at 2,800 feet (853 m). Water emerges at 50 degrees Fahrenheit (10°C).

Graglia,
ITALY

CARBONATION 10 mg/l artificial TDS 14 mg/l HARDNESS 4 mg/l pH 5.75 NITRATE 1.4 mg/l CALCIUM 1 mg/l MAGNESIUM 0.3 mg/l SODIUM 1 mg/l POTASSIUM 0.3 mg/l SILICA 5 mg/l BICARBONATE 4 mg/l SULFATES 2 mg/l CHLORIDES 0.5 mg/l

VIRGINALITY: ♦ ♦ ♦ ♦

REGION: Piedmont

SOURCE: Spring at 3,300 feet (1,005 m)

MINERALITY: Super Low

HARDNESS: Soft

ORIENTATION: Acidic

VINTAGE: 1 year

LE BLEU

Established 1990

STILL

The taste of Le Bleu is, simply put, that of one oxygen and two hydrogen molecules—there is nothing else in the water. A curiosity for the water connoisseur and useful to calibrate one's palate in a water tasting. Great for making transparent ice cubes.

No minerals or trace elements remain in Le Bleu after the company's five-step purification process. Steam distillation is one of the steps used to bring the water to an ultra-pure TDS of 0 mg/l. The available blue plastic (PET) bottle is at home in an epicurean setting.

Advance,
USA

TDS 0 mg/l **HARDNESS** 0 mg/l **pH** 7 **NITRATE** 0 mg/l **CALCIUM** 0 mg/l **MAGNESIUM** 0 mg/l **SODIUM** 0 mg/l **POTASSIUM** 0 mg/l **SILICA** 0 mg/l **BICARBONATE** 0 mg/l **SULFATES** 0 mg/l **CHLORIDES** 0 mg/l

VIRGINALITY: ♦ ♦ ♦ ♦ ♦
REGION: North Carolina
SOURCE: Processed
MINERALITY: Super Low
HARDNESS: Soft
ORIENTATION: Neutral

LEVISSIMA

Established 1964

STILL   EFFERVESCENT

Usually consumed in its Still version as a sports and fitness drink, this water is seldom seen in the context of fine dining. However, the carbonated version is very nice for mixed drinks. Levissima has a dedicated following.

This low TDS water emerges at 46 degrees Fahrenheit (8°C) from a spring high in the Italian Alps, near the Bormio ski resort. Pipes lined with glass then carry the water down to the bottling facility in the valley. With an especially wide distribution in northern Italy, Levissima is very popular throughout the country.

Levissima,
Italy

CARBONATION 1.4 mg/l artificial **TDS** 76 mg/l **HARDNESS** 58 mg/l **pH** 7.6 **NITRATE** 1.6 mg/l **CALCIUM** 20 mg/l **MAGNESIUM** 2 mg/l **SODIUM** 2 mg/l **POTASSIUM** 2 mg/l **SILICA** 6 mg/l **BICARBONATE** 57 mg/l **SULFATES** 14 mg/l **CHLORIDES** <1 mg/l

VIRGINALITY: ◆ ◆ ◆ ◆
REGION: Valdisotto, Italian Alps
SOURCE: Spring at 6,160 feet (1,878 m)
MINERALITY: Low
HARDNESS: Slightly Hard
ORIENTATION: Hint of Sweet

LLANLLYR SOURCE

ESTABLISHED 1999

STILL EFFERVESCENT

This water has a low mineral content, a low nitrate level, and an acidic pH. I liked the original bottle for Llanllyr Source Premium, but it was probably not cost-effective. The new bottle design was introduced in 2004.

A single family has farmed the unspoiled fields around the Llanllyr source since 1720. The water is extracted from Llandovery shale, a fine gravel left behind by glaciers retreating from the valley. A Cistercian nunnery obtained its water more than eight hundred years ago from the same source used today. The much-admired first Llanllyr bottle won an international award for its design, though the current, contemporary bottle dates from 2004.

Llanllyr,
UNITED KINGDOM

CARBONATION artificial TDS 84 mg/l HARDNESS 54 mg/l
pH 6.1 NITRATE <1 mg/l CALCIUM 12 mg/l MAGNESIUM
6 mg/l SODIUM 14 mg/l POTASSIUM 2 mg/l BICARBONATE
68 mg/l SULFATES 17 mg/l CHLORIDES 30 mg/l

VIRGINALITY: ♦ ♦ ♦ ♦ ♦
REGION: West Wales
SOURCE: Well
MINERALITY: Low
HARDNESS: Slightly Hard
ORIENTATION: Acidic

LURISIA
(SANTA BARBARA)
Established 1917

STILL | CLASSIC

This respected Piedmont water is one of the lowest mineral content waters in Italy. It has a very light and neutral taste. I love the 1950s design of the bottle and label as well as the traditional crown cap and the company's commitment to glass bottles. The sparkling version is perfect for mixed drinks.

While water emerges cold from two of the Alpine site's four springs, Santa Barbara and Acquam Spring, the others, Garbarino and Santa Barbara Grotta, are hot springs. Marie Curie was the first to study the health benefits of water from the Garbarino spring in 1918—water that today may only be prescribed by the nearby spa. Water emerges from the Santa Barbara spring at 49 degrees Fahrenheit (9°C).

Fonte S. Barbara di
Lurisia, ITALY

CARBONATION 7.5 mg/l artificial **TDS** 35 mg/l **HARDNESS** 10 mg/l **pH** 6.9 **NITRATE** 2.2 mg/l **CALCIUM** 3.3 mg/l **MAGNESIUM** <1 mg/l **SODIUM** 3 mg/l **POTASSIUM** 1 mg/l **SILICA** 14 mg/l **BICARBONATE** 15 mg/l **SULFATES** 2 mg/l **CHLORIDES** <1 mg/l

VIRGINALITY: ◆ ◆ ◆ ◆
REGION: Piedmont
SOURCE: Spring at 5,100 feet (1,555 m)
MINERALITY: Super Low
HARDNESS: Soft
ORIENTATION: Neutral

LYNX

STILL

LIGHT

Lynx is one of the elite Italian waters. The striking cobalt blue bottle brings class to any table or bar.

Rough terrain and tall trees protect the Lynx source on the northeastern face of the 4,900-foot (1,490 m) Mount Pelpi, near the small town of Bedonia. Water surfaces at 45 degrees Fahrenheit (7°C) and is carried by gravity through 6,400 feet (1,950 m) of stainless steel pipeline to the bottling facility in a more accessible location.

Fonti di San Fermo,
ITALY

CARBONATION 4.5 mg/l artificial TDS 163 mg/l HARDNESS 148 mg/l pH 7.6 NITRATE 3.3 mg/l CALCIUM 52 mg/l MAGNESIUM 4 mg/l SODIUM 3 mg/l SILICA 5 mg/l BICARBONATE

VIRGINALITY: ♦ ♦ ♦ ♦

REGION: Parma

SOURCE: Spring at 3,650 feet (1,112 m)

MINERALITY: Low

HARDNESS: Hard

ORIENTATION: Neutral

MALAVELLA

Established 1829

STILL   CLASSIC

This very high TDS water has a neutral pH and significant levels of bicarbonate and sodium. Malavella is very similar to Vichy Catalan.

Construction of a mine first uncovered the spring, then called La Mina, in 1829. The spring provided local spas with mineral water, which was also bottled exclusively for the spa-goers. Wider commercial sales began in 1940 under the brand Font de la Mina. Malavella, which emerges at 134 degrees Fahrenheit (57°C), comes from the same aquifer as Vichy Catalan—the waters are similar but composed slightly differently.

Caldes de Malavella, Spain

CARBONATION artificial **TDS** 3,049 mg/l **HARDNESS** 171 mg/l **pH** 6.92 **NITRATE** <1 mg/l **CALCIUM** 54 mg/l **MAGNESIUM** 9 mg/l **SODIUM** 1,115 mg/l **POTASSIUM** 49 mg/l **SILICA** 77 mg/l **BICARBONATE** 2214 mg/l **SULFATES** 48 mg/l **CHLORIDES** 594 mg/l

VIRGINALITY: ♦ ♦ ♦ ♦ ♦
REGION: Girona
SOURCE: Spring
MINERALITY: Very High
HARDNESS: Hard
ORIENTATION: Neutral

MALMBERG

Established 1990

STILL   LIGHT

This very stylish, lightly carbonated, alkaline water comes from a pristine source and is high in bicarbonate. Perfect for a well-laid dinner table.

Rain falling in beech forests on southern Sweden's Linderöd Ridge spent five thousand years being filtered by earth, clay, rock, and limestone before accumulating 12 miles (20 km) east of the ridge. Artesian pressure brings 48 gallons (182 l) of water per minute to the surface through a borehole drilled in 1990.

Yngsjö,
SWEDEN

CARBONATION 3.8 mg/l artificial **TDS** 220 mg/l **HARDNESS** 190 mg/l **pH** 8.2 **NITRATE** <1 mg/l **CALCIUM** 68 mg/l **MAGNESIUM** 5 mg/l **SODIUM** 6 mg/l **POTASSIUM** 2 mg/l **BICARBONATE** 220 mg/l **SULFATES** 6 mg/l **CHLORIDES** 8 mg/l

VIRGINALITY: ♦ ♦ ♦ ♦ ♦
REGION: Skåne County
SOURCE: Artesian
MINERALITY: Low
HARDNESS: Very Hard
ORIENTATION: Alkaline
VINTAGE: 5,245 years

MANITOU

ESTABLISHED 1872

STILL

Manitou is a very high mineral content water with a significant level of bicarbonate. Manitou can also be a significant source of calcium. It's a substantial water that draws attention.

Manitou gains a high TDS in the earth before natural artesian pressure at the Ute Chief Gusher brings the water to the surface. Manitou Springs were held sacred by the Ute, Arapaho, Cheyenne, and Kiowa nations of Native Americans long before doctors began prescribing the water about 110 years ago. Theodore Roosevelt, Thomas Edison, and William Henry Jackson were known to enjoy the waters.

Manitou Springs,
USA

TDS 1,600 mg/l **HARDNESS** 829 mg/l **pH** 6.6 **NITRATE** 6.7 mg/l **CALCIUM** 296 mg/l **MAGNESIUM** 52 mg/l **SODIUM** 136 mg/l **POTASSIUM** 19 mg/l **BICARBONATE** 1,000 mg/l **SULFATES** 84 mg/l **CHLORIDES** 87 mg/l

VIRGINALITY: ◆ ◆ ◆

REGION: Colorado

SOURCE: Artesian

MINERALITY: Very High

HARDNESS: Very Hard

ORIENTATION: Acidic

MONDARIZ

Established 1878

STILL

This slightly acidic, low minerality water is one of the leading brands in northern Spain and Portugal. It is available in glass or plastic.

Known since the Roman period, the water started being bottled in the late nineteenth century to spread the curative benefits farther afield. Before the spa baths were built, health-seekers drank the water, which surfaces at 63 degrees Fahrenheit (17°C). The water is bottled just over a mile (2 km) from the source.

Mondariz,
Spain

TDS 160 mg/l HARDNESS 58 mg/l pH 6.56 NITRATE <1 mg/l
CALCIUM 12 mg/l MAGNESIUM 7 mg/l SODIUM 39 mg/l
POTASSIUM 3 mg/l SULFATES 2 mg/l CHLORIDES 12 mg/l

VIRGINALITY: ♦ ♦ ♦ ♦ ♦
REGION: Pontevedra
SOURCE: Spring
MINERALITY: Low
HARDNESS: Slightly Hard
ORIENTATION: Acidic
VINTAGE: 150 years

MONTAQUA

ESTABLISHED 1999

STILL

This little-known American water rivals many imports. The medium TDS water also features an extremely low nitrate level and a pH that sometimes hints at sweetness. I would love to see this water in a nice glass bottle for a more upscale presentation.

Though Native Americans had long known the healing benefits of the spring's water, Lewis and Clark were the first to document it, in 1805. The curative value of the water for "pleasure seekers and invalids" was noted in an 1881 *Dillon Tribune* article. Geothermal pressure brings the water up from the ground all year at a constant rate of more than 700,000 gallons (2.65 million l) each day. The first test of the source ten miles (16 km) south of Dillon, Montana, was carried out in 1990.

Dillon,
USA

TDS 420 mg/l **HARDNESS** 290 mg/l **pH** 7.3 **NITRATE** <1 mg/l
CALCIUM 72 mg/l **MAGNESIUM** 24 mg/l **SODIUM** 22 mg/l
POTASSIUM 4 mg/l **SULFATES** 130 mg/l **CHLORIDES** 10 mg/l

VIRGINALITY: ◆◆◆◆◆

REGION: Montana

SOURCE: Artesian

MINERALITY: Medium

HARDNESS: Very Hard

ORIENTATION: Neutral

MOUNTAIN VALLEY SPRING

STILL   CLASSIC

ESTABLISHED 1871

I love Mountain Valley Spring's dedication to glass bottles and the low mineral content water that comes in them. The 130-year-old company calls its product "America's Premium Water."

The bottling company owns 633 acres (256 hectares) of forest surrounding the spring near Hot Springs National Park. Shale, sandstone, and limestone impart minerals such as calcium, magnesium, and trace elements during the water's 3,500-year journey to the spring.

Hot Springs, USA

CARBONATION 5.4 mg/l artificial **TDS** 221 mg/l **HARDNESS** 210 mg/l **pH** 7.7 **NITRATE** <1 mg/l **CALCIUM** 71 mg/l **MAGNESIUM** 8 mg/l **SODIUM** 3 mg/l **POTASSIUM** 1 mg/l **SILICA** 5 mg/l **BICARBONATE** 176 mg/l **SULFATES** 9 mg/l **CHLORIDES** 4 mg/l

VIRGINALITY: ◆ ◆ ◆ ◆ ◆
REGION: Arkansas
SOURCE: Spring
MINERALITY: Low
HARDNESS: Very Hard
ORIENTATION: Hint of Sweet
VINTAGE: 3,500 years

MOUNT OLYMPUS

Established 1898

Mount Olympus water has a very low mineral content. The water has huge potential for epicurean use, but unfortunately it's only available in plastic. Mount Olympus is a great water disguised as commodity water.

The spring is found on federally protected land in Neff's Canyon. The water has been studied for more than fifty years, with a remarkably consistent and uniform composition through the decades, and it is not treated with chlorine or other additives. The bottling company capped the spring and tanks the water to a plant above Mount Olympus Cove, where it is bottled.

Mount Olympus
Spring, USA

TDS 54 mg/l **HARDNESS** 32 mg/l **pH** 6.5 **NITRATE** <1 mg/l
CALCIUM 9 mg/l **MAGNESIUM** 3 mg/l **SODIUM** 6 mg/l
POTASSIUM <1 mg/l **SULFATES** 11 mg/l **CHLORIDES** 6 mg/l

VIRGINALITY: ♦ ♦ ♦ ♦ ♦
REGION: Salt Lake City, Utah
SOURCE: Spring at 5,000 feet (1,524 m)
MINERALITY: Low
HARDNESS: Slightly Hard
ORIENTATION: Acidic

1 LITRE

<small>ESTABLISHED 2004</small>

The perfect water to drink at the pool of a fancy resort or—if you must—on the go, 1 Litre comes in a stylish plastic bottle with a built-in cup. Why didn't anyone think of that before?

Several systems of streams that empty into Lake Ontario have their headwaters in Ontario province's Oak Ridges Moraine, which is also home to one of the world's largest aquifers. The spring used by 1 Litre is in the Northumberland County Forest, a part of the Moraine that enjoys government protection. The water is bottled at the source after multiple filtrations to remove particles larger than 0.2 microns and disinfected by ultraviolet light and ozonation.

Northumberland Forest, CANADA

TDS 233 mg/l **HARDNESS** 174 mg/l **pH** 7.9 **NITRATE** <1 mg/l **CALCIUM** 46 mg/l **MAGNESIUM** 14 mg/l **SODIUM** 2 mg/l **POTASSIUM** 1 mg/l **BICARBONATE** 176 mg/l **SULFATES** 22 mg/l **CHLORIDES** 2 mg/l

VIRGINALITY: ◆ ◆ ◆ ◆ ◆
REGION: Oak Ridges Moraine, Ontario
SOURCE: Spring
MINERALITY: Low
HARDNESS: Hard
ORIENTATION: Alkaline

OREGON RAIN

ESTABLISHED 2004

STILL

Soft and super low mineral content rainwater. This is a very nice alternative to aquifer based, low mineral content waters. The perfect match for very subtle mouthfeel dishes or enjoyed on its own based on a great story and unique terroir.

Before founding Oregon Rain in 2004, Dan McGee distributed bottles of rainwater to people he knew. They all had something positive to say about the water, so commercial sales began. Because the water is collected as soon as it falls from the sky, with no interference from the earth, the company refers to the water as "Virgin Water." The collection sheets are sterile, but filtration and pasteurization keep the water homogeneous. No arsenic, chlorine, chromium-6, MTBE, fluoride, or nitrates are present.

Newberg, USA

TDS 11 mg/l HARDNESS 0 mg/l pH 7.4 NITRATE 0 mg/l CALCIUM 0 mg/l MAGNESIUM 0 mg/l SODIUM 0 mg/l POTASSIUM 0 mg/l SILICA 0 mg/l BICARBONATE 0 mg/l SULFATES 0 mg/l CHLORIDES 0 mg/l

VIRGINALITY: ♦ ♦ ♦ ♦

REGION: Oregon

SOURCE: Rain

MINERALITY: Super Low

HARDNESS: Soft

ORIENTATION: Hint of Sweet

VINTAGE: I week

PANNA

Established 1927

STILL

Be prepared to see this moderately hard, low TDS water more and more in restaurants as the "still" water in your "still or sparkling" choice. Panna, with its slightly alkaline taste, is distributed by Nestlé, which also brings you San Pellegrino.

Nobles, shepherds, and other locals have for centuries recognized the quality of this water from the Tuscan Apennines. According to legend, the spring, now sur-rounded by a nature reserve, offered a refreshing stop on the only ancient Roman road linking the north and south of Italy.

Villa Panna,
ITALY

TDS 188 mg/l HARDNESS 103 mg/l pH 8.2 NITRATE 5.7 mg/l CALCIUM 30 mg/l MAGNESIUM 7 mg/l SODIUM 7 mg/l POTASSIUM 1 mg/l SILICA 8 mg/l BICARBONATE 100 mg/l SULFATES 21 mg/l CHLORIDES 7 mg/l

VIRGINALITY: ◆ ◆ ◆

REGION: Tuscany

SOURCE: Spring at 3,700 feet (1,127 m)

MINERALITY: Low

HARDNESS: Moderately Hard

ORIENTATION: Alkaline

PELAGONIA

ESTABLISHED 1992

STILL · LIGHT

Pelagonia is a soft water with a very high pH. It is a unique water from a pristine source.

The Macedonian source was known in the time of Alexander the Great; the water emerging from the 2,300-foot-deep (700 m) geothermal artesian spring can be carbon dated to more than one thousand years. Mountain rock 60 miles (96 km) from the Mediterranean coast filters the water; the region is free of industrial pollution. Along with its high pH of 9.4, Pelagonia is remarkable for containing selenium, a rare mineral.

Devin,
BULGARIA

CARBONATION artificial TDS 159 mg/l HARDNESS 10 mg/l
pH 9.4 NITRATE <1 mg/l CALCIUM 1 mg/l MAGNESIUM 1 mg/l
SODIUM 60 mg/l POTASSIUM 2 mg/l BICARBONATE 86 mg/l
SILICA 40 mg/l SULFATES 20 mg/l CHLORIDES 3 mg/l

VIRGINALITY: ◆ ◆ ◆ ◆ ◆
REGION: Rhodope Mountains
SOURCE: Artesian
MINERALITY: Low
HARDNESS: Soft
ORIENTATION: Alkaline
VINTAGE: 1,000 years

PERRIER

ESTABLISHED 1863

BOLD

The big, loud bubbles create a "fireworks in your mouth" sensation. Perrier has a very high level of nitrate and a very acidic pH. Perrier's famous marquee enjoys a perception of prestige and privilege.

Perrier has been imported into the United States for about a century. The water's popularity in the U.S. market truly took off amid the healthy-living boom of the late 1970s. Thanks to the marketing efforts of Nestlé Waters North America, Perrier became an attractive natural alternative to less-healthful alcohol and soft drinks. Though still bottled at its original site, the water and carbon dioxide are now harvested from separate underground locations and combined during bottling.

Vergèze, FRANCE

CARBONATION natural TDS 475 mg/l HARDNESS 380 mg/l pH 5.5 NITRATE 4.3 mg/l CALCIUM 147 mg/l MAGNESIUM 3 mg/l SODIUM 9 mg/l POTASSIUM 1 mg/l BICARBONATE 390 mg/l SULFATES 33 mg/l CHLORIDES 22 mg/l

VIRGINALITY: ♦ ♦ ♦

REGION: Arles

SOURCE: Spring

MINERALITY: Medium

HARDNESS: Very Hard

ORIENTATION: Acidic

QUARZIA

STILL   BOLD

The elegant, pyramid-shaped bottle resembles a high-end grappa bottle —fitting for a water that comes from a vineyard producing the high-proof alcohol. Quarzia would be perfect for diluting grappa if it weren't for the water's elevated nitrate level.

Distilleria Bottega has produced wine and grappa for three generations and recently began bottling a light mountain water from two springs in an Alpine valley 2,950 feet (900 m) above sea level. The water has a low mineral content.

Fonte Paraviso,
ITALY

CARBONATION 10 mg/l artificial **TDS** 226 mg/l **HARDNESS** 204 mg/l **pH** 7.5 **NITRATE** 11.8 mg/l **CALCIUM** 69 mg/l **MAGNESIUM** 8 mg/l **SODIUM** 1 mg/l **POTASSIUM** 1 mg/l **SILICA** 7 mg/l **SULFATES** 8 mg/l **CHLORIDES** 3 mg/l

VIRGINALITY: ◆

REGION: Lanzo d'Intelvi

SOURCE: Spring at 2,800 feet (850 m)

MINERALITY: Low

HARDNESS: Very Hard

ORIENTATION: Hint of Sweet

RADENSKA

This very high mineral content water has high levels of bicarbonate, calcium, and potassium. Radenska has a distinct mineral taste and a soft feeling for such a hard water. The naturally sparkling mineral water is considered a sophisticated curative, giving it a European character.

Three mineral springs near the border between Austria and Slovenia supply Radenska: Miral, Radin, and Vrelec. The aquifer is at a shallow depth; deeper volcanic activity lends a natural sparkle to the water. In 1833, Karel Henn became the first to attribute health benefits to the water, which began being bottled in earthen jars in 1869. Visitors to the spa in Radenci have enjoyed the water's curative properties since 1882.

Kraljevi Vrelec,
SLOVENIA

CARBONATION 3.5 mg/l natural TDS 3,262 mg/l HARDNESS 923 mg/l pH 6.3 NITRATE 2 mg/l CALCIUM 230 mg/l MAGNESIUM 87 mg/l SODIUM 390 mg/l POTASSIUM 64 mg/l SILICA 70 mg/l BICARBONATE 2,370 mg/l SULFATES 76 mg/l CHLORIDES 44 mg/l

VIRGINALITY: ♦ ♦ ♦ ♦
REGION: Radenci
SOURCE: Spring
MINERALITY: Very High
HARDNESS: Very Hard
ORIENTATION: Acidic

RAMLÖSA

ESTABLISHED 1707

STILL   LIGHT

In Sweden, Ramlösa is almost the definition of mineral water. I love this refreshing water, with its hint of sour, medium mineral content, and light carbonation. Ramlösa is a very soft water with a high level of sodium, which can produce a salty perception.

During the eighteenth and nineteenth centuries, Ramlösa was among northern Europe's most elite spas; drinking the water was also thought to have a therapeutic value. While making a 70-year, 270-foot (82 m) journey to the aquifer, the water is filtered and enriched with minerals by twenty layers of sandstone, clay, coal, and sand. Before bottling, the water is only aerated, filtered, and carbonated.

Ramlösa,
SWEDEN

CARBONATION 5 mg/l artificial TDS 520 mg/l HARDNESS 8 mg/l pH 5.6 NITRATE NA CALCIUM 2 mg/l MAGNESIUM <1 mg/l SODIUM 222 mg/l POTASSIUM 2 mg/l BICARBONATE 12 mg/l SULFATES 7 mg/l CHLORIDES 23 mg/l

VIRGINALITY: Not Available

REGION: Hälsbronn, Helsingborg

SOURCE: Spring

MINERALITY: Medium

HARDNESS: Soft

ORIENTATION: Acidic

VINTAGE: 70 years

RÖMERQUELLE

Established 1925

STILL · LIGHT · CLASSIC

One of the most prominent brands in Austria, Römerquelle is widely used in spritzer. The three different versions of the water—still (no carbonation), mild (moderate carbonation levels) and prickelned (high carbonation levels)—allow for fine-tuning the water to various foods.

Many of the best-known Central European spas, such as Karlsbad, Marienbad, Bad Vöslau, and Radenska, are located along the Thermenline thermal line, created by tectonic forces millions of years ago. Artesian pressure brings Römerquelle water to the surface along one of the thermal line's offshoots; the water emerges at 63 degrees Fahrenheit (17°C). Geological strata there filter rainwater for 5,300 years.

Edelstal,
Austria

CARBONATION 2–3 mg/l, 5–6 mg/l artificial **TDS** 1,000 mg/l **HARDNESS** 630 mg/l **pH** NA **NITRATE** <1 mg/l **CALCIUM** 146 mg/l **MAGNESIUM** 66 mg/l **SODIUM** 14 mg/l **POTASSIUM** 2 mg/l **BICARBONATE** 421 mg/l **SULFATES** 299 mg/l **CHLORIDES** 8 mg/l

VIRGINALITY: ♦ ♦ ♦ ♦ ♦

REGION: Burgenland

SOURCE: Artesian

MINERALITY: High

HARDNESS: Very Hard

ORIENTATION: Acidic

VINTAGE: 5,300 years

SAINT-ÉLIE

STILL

This water spends about sixty years in very hard crystalline rocks at an elevated temperature, resulting in a surprisingly low mineral content and a high pH.

An impermeable layer of thick clay protects the spring from surface pollutants. Precambrian, crystalline rocks—some of the oldest on the planet—form the area from which the aquifer draws its water. There is very little habitation in the 385,000 square miles (1 million sq km) of territory surrounding the source. Water surfaces at 41 degrees Fahrenheit (5°C).

Saint-Élie-de-Caxton,
CANADA

TDS 174 mg/l HARDNESS 60 mg/l pH 8.2 NITRATE <1 mg/l
CALCIUM 16 mg/l MAGNESIUM 5 mg/l SODIUM 44 mg/l
POTASSIUM 4 mg/l BICARBONATE 100 mg/l SULFATES 7 mg/l
CHLORIDES 21 mg/l

VIRGINALITY: ◆ ◆ ◆ ◆ ◆
REGION: Québec
SOURCE: Spring
MINERALITY: Low
HARDNESS: Slightly Hard
ORIENTATION: Alkaline
VINTAGE: 60 years

SAINT-JUSTIN

ESTABLISHED 1971

STILL

BOLD

A robust and surprisingly soft water, Saint-Justin's high mineral content includes significant amounts of bicarbonate and sodium but very little calcium and magnesium.

The mineral water is bottled at the source in the lower Laurentian Mountains. Clay, sand, and gravel between the surface and the 150-foot-deep (46 m) spring filter the water.

Saint-Justin,
CANADA

CARBONATION artificial **TDS** 1,000 mg/l **HARDNESS** 42 mg/l
pH 8 **NITRATE** <1 mg/l **CALCIUM** 7 mg/l **MAGNESIUM** 6 mg/l
SODIUM 415 mg/l **POTASSIUM** 3 mg/l **SILICA** 0 mg/l
BICARBONATE 560 mg/l **SULFATES** 0 mg/l **CHLORIDES** 350 mg/l

VIRGINALITY: ♦ ♦ ♦ ♦ ♦
REGION: Québec
SOURCE: Spring
MINERALITY: High
HARDNESS: Slightly Hard
ORIENTATION: Alkaline

SAN BENEDETTO

STILL

BOLD

This low mineral content, slightly alkaline, but very hard water has a nice measure of bicarbonate (which makes it good for digestion). Artificial carbonation makes a sparkling water with a Bold designation, which feels less carbonated than the numbers suggest.

Aristocratic families of ninth- through eighteenth-century Venice highly regarded this water, which originally comes from glaciers in the Dolomites. Though the water used to be collected at the surface, San Benedetto is now taken from 1,000 feet (305 m) underground to preserve its natural composition. The water surfaces with a temperature of 62 degrees Fahrenheit (17°C).

Scorze,
ITALY

CARBONATION 12 mg/l artificial TDS 250 mg/l HARDNESS 235 mg/l pH 7.7 NITRATE 6.8 mg/l CALCIUM 46 mg/l MAGNESIUM 30 mg/l SODIUM 7 mg/l POTASSIUM 1 mg/l SILICA 17 mg/l BICARBONATE 293 mg/l SULFATES 5 mg/l CHLORIDES 3 mg/l

VIRGINALITY: ◆ ◆ ◆

REGION: Veneto

SOURCE: Artesian

MINERALITY: Low

HARDNESS: Very Hard

ORIENTATION: Hint of Sweet

SANFAUSTINO

ESTABLISHED 1894

EFFERVESCENT

Sanfaustino is remarkable for its unique combination of high calcium and low sodium content (it qualifies as sodium-free under USFDA regulations) coupled with a very low level of natural carbonation. This substantial water is best for dishes with subtle mouthfeel that might otherwise be served with red wine. Sanfaustino is not recommended for mixed drinks.

A family-owned company has bottled Sanfaustino for 110 years. Fissures in the earth's surface impart a natural carbonation to the water. Calcium is dissolved into the water from travertine rock—the water's pH, temperature, and pressure aid the process.

Massa Martana, ITALY

CARBONATION natural **TDS** 1,170 mg/l **HARDNESS** 1,101 mg/l **pH** 5.9 **NITRATE** 1.4 mg/l **CALCIUM** 450 mg/l **MAGNESIUM** 19 mg/l **SODIUM** 21 mg/l **POTASSIUM** 3 mg/l **SILICA** 15 mg/l **BICARBONATE** 950 mg/l **SULFATES** 72 mg/l **CHLORIDES** 19 mg/l

VIRGINALITY: ◆ ◆ ◆ ◆
REGION: Umbria
SOURCE: Spring
MINERALITY: High
HARDNESS: Very Hard
ORIENTATION: Acidic

SAN PELLEGRINO

ESTABLISHED 1899

Although it is exported widely, San Pellegrino is not common in Italy. The water's greatest asset is its very low nitrate level, which indicates an unspoiled source. This high mineral content water is also a fairly significant source of sulfates and calcium. It is a nice water, but I'd love to see alternatives in restaurants.

The sumptuous marble drinking hall Fonte Termale stands in the town of San Pellegrino as a reminder of "taking the waters" in a bygone era. Three 1,300-foot-deep (396 m) springs bring the still water to the surface at 78.6 degrees Fahrenheit (26°C). San Pellegrino was first put on the map when Leonardo da Vinci sampled the town's waters.

San Pellegrino Terme,
ITALY

CARBONATION artificial TDS 1,109 mg/l HARDNESS 744 mg/l pH 7.7 NITRATE <1 mg/l CALCIUM 208 mg/l MAGNESIUM 56 mg/l SODIUM 44 mg/l POTASSIUM 3 mg/l BICARBONATE 136 mg/l SULFATES 549 mg/l CHLORIDES 74 mg/l

VIRGINALITY: ♦ ♦ ♦ ♦ ♦
REGION: Milan
SOURCE: Spring
MINERALITY: High
HARDNESS: Very Hard
ORIENTATION: Hint of Sweet

SANTA CROCE

ESTABLISHED 1975

STILL | LIGHT

This water comes from a pristine source. The light but hard water has very low levels of minerals and is basically sodium free. I like the blue plastic bottle for its upscale look.

The Romans knew Santa Croce's Sponga spring, which is now surrounded by nationally protected parkland in the Apennine Mountains. Small cascades and pools are created by the steady flow of the spring water, which emerges at 44 degrees Fahrenheit (7°C). Very popular in Italy, Santa Croce is bottled in a variety of plastic and glass packages and sold as a private-label water on cruise lines and in other parts of the hospitality industry.

Santa Croce,
ITALY

CARBONATION 4 mg/l artificial **TDS** 170 mg/l **HARDNESS** 140 mg/l **pH** 7.84 **NITRATE** <1 mg/l **CALCIUM** 48 mg/l **MAGNESIUM** 5 mg/l **SODIUM** 1 mg/l **POTASSIUM** <1 mg/l **SILICA** 2 mg/l **BICARBONATE** 195 mg/l **SULFATES** 1 mg/l **CHLORIDES** 7 mg/l

VIRGINALITY: ♦ ♦ ♦ ♦ ♦

REGION: Abruzzo

SOURCE: Spring at 2,500 feet (762 m)

MINERALITY: Low

HARDNESS: Hard

ORIENTATION: Alkaline

SARATOGA

ESTABLISHED 1872

STILL | BOLD

*Often overlooked by the hospital-
ity industry, Saratoga Spring Water
is a nice epicurean alternative to
imported, high-end, glass-bottled
mineral water. The carbonation is
bold with a lot of "fizz." Perfect
for food with a strong mouthfeel,
the water can also be enjoyed with
appetizers as a champagne replace-
ment. I love the blue bottle.*

The Iroquois were the first to
experience the healing benefits of
Saratoga Springs, which they discovered in the fourteenth century.
European settlers found a similar
value in the mineral waters, and
the luxury resort built around the
springs grew to be one of
America's most esteemed spas.
Bottling of the water began in
1872 on the same site used by the
current plant.

Saratoga Springs,
USA

CARBONATION artificial TDS 73 mg/l HARDNESS 36 mg/l
pH 6.98 NITRATE <1 mg/l CALCIUM 11 mg/l MAGNESIUM
2 mg/l SODIUM 7 mg/l POTASSIUM <1 mg/l BICARBONATE
26 mg/l SULFATES 7 mg/l CHLORIDES 10 mg/l

VIRGINALITY: ◆ ◆ ◆ ◆ ◆

REGION: Adirondacks, New York

SOURCE: Spring

MINERALITY: Light

HARDNESS: Slightly Hard

ORIENTATION: Alkaline

SEAWRIGHT SPRINGS

STILL

ESTABLISHED 1741

The source of this medium mineral content water has a long history. The water is extremely low in sodium; it features a very beneficial 1:2 ratio of magnesium to calcium and comes in an upscale plastic bottle.

Native Americans knew of this source of "good health water" and showed it to European explorers. John Seawright acquired the spring in 1741; it is now surrounded by federally protected forest. Every day, more than one million gallons (3.8 million l) flow at a constant 59 degrees Fahrenheit (15°C) to a circular pool 1,000 feet (305 m) above the aquifer.

Augusta County, USA

TDS 300 mg/l **HARDNESS** 180 mg/l **pH** 7.34 **NITRATE** 2.5 mg/l **CALCIUM** 70 mg/l **MAGNESIUM** 32 mg/l **SODIUM** 1 mg/l **POTASSIUM** 2 mg/l **BICARBONATE** 250 mg/l **SULFATES** 6 mg/l **CHLORIDES** 4 mg/l

VIRGINALITY: ♦ ♦ ♦ ♦

REGION: Virginia

SOURCE: Spring

MINERALITY: Medium

HARDNESS: Hard

ORIENTATION: Hint of Sweet

SELTERS

ESTABLISHED 1896

STILL

LIGHT

BOLD

The town of Selters is immortalized in the generic terms for carbonated water, Selters water or seltzer. Today, the bottler carries on a classic European tradition by artificially carbonating the very high TDS water to Light and Bold levels.

The village of Selters gets its name from the Celtic word for the springs, Saltarissa. The naturally carbonated water, one of Europe's oldest brands, was sold widely in stone jars until the flow of the springs stopped in the nineteenth century. To restore the flow, a 1,000-foot (305 m) artesian well was drilled in 1896. This well was known as Auguste Victoria after the German empress of the same name. The stone jars of the past served as a model for today's remarkable blue bottle.

Selters an der Lahn,
GERMANY

CARBONATION 8.2 mg/l, 4.5 mg/l artificial TDS 1,610 mg/l HARDNESS NA pH NA NITRATE NA CALCIUM 110 mg/l MAGNESIUM 40 mg/l SODIUM 290 mg/l POTASSIUM 13 mg/l SILICA NA BICARBONATE 850 mg/l SULFATES 20 mg/l CHLORIDES 260 mg/l

VIRGINALITY: Not Available

REGION: Löhnberg

SOURCE: Well

MINERALITY: Very High

HARDNESS: Very High

ORIENTATION: Not Available

SOLÉ

STILL

CLASSIC

Some people find Solé to be a little sweet, especially in its Still version. The water has an interesting combination of high bicarbonate and low sodium levels in a medium minerality water, and artificial carbonation adds a Light version to the line. Restaurants often offer Solé as an alternative to the much heavier and more alkaline San Pellegrino.

The water's curative effects were famed in the medieval period, but the source had been known by the Romans. The statue of a pagan sun goddess once stood there, according to archaeological research, and the name Solé suggests this connection to the sun. A family-operated company bottles the water at its Lombard source near the Alps.

Nuvolento,
ITALY

CARBONATION 5.5 mg/l artificial **TDS** 400 mg/l **HARDNESS** 394 mg/l **pH** 7.4 **NITRATE** <1 mg/l **CALCIUM** 108 mg/l **MAGNESIUM** 31 mg/l **SODIUM** 2 mg/l **POTASSIUM** 43 mg/l **SILICA** 6 mg/l **BICARBONATE** 440 mg/l **SULFATES** 19 mg/l **CHLORIDES** 3 mg/l

VIRGINALITY: ♦ ♦ ♦ ♦ ♦
REGION: Lombardia
SOURCE: Spring
MINERALITY: Medium
HARDNESS: Very Hard
ORIENTATION: Hint of Sweet

SPA

ESTABLISHED 1583

STILL | LIGHT

Very low levels of calcium and magnesium make Spa a soft water with a slight hint of sourness. The very clean-tasting water is also low in minerals and sodium. Spa is a perfect match for dishes with the most subtle mouthfeel. I love it with sushi, sashimi, and other raw seafood.

The Spa springs, protected from pollution by the Ardennes Mountains nature reserve, bring water with a light carbonation to the surface. The sparkling Spa Marie-Henriette water, however, is not as popular as the Spa Reine still water.

Spa,
BELGIUM

SPA REINE: **TDS** 33 mg/l **HARDNESS** 16 mg/l **pH** 6 **NITRATE** 1.9 mg/l **CALCIUM** 5 mg/l **MAGNESIUM** 1 mg/l **SODIUM** 3 mg/l **POTASSIUM** <1 mg/l **SILICA** 7 mg/l **BICARBONATE** 15 mg/l **SULFATES** 4 mg/l **CHLORIDES** 5 mg/l

SPA MARIE-HENRIETTE: **CARBONATION** 3.8 mg/l natural **TDS** 95 mg/l **HARDNESS** 17 mg/l **pH** 6 **NITRATE** <1 mg/l **CALCIUM** 11 mg/l **MAGNESIUM** 7 mg/l **SODIUM** 11 mg/l **POTASSIUM** 1 mg/l **SILICA** 15 mg/l **BICARBONATE** 75 mg/l **SULFATES** 7 mg/l **CHLORIDES** 10 mg/l

VIRGINALITY: ◆ ◆ ◆ ◆
REGION: Ardennes
SOURCE: Spring at 1,440 feet (439 m)
MINERALITY: Super Low
HARDNESS: Soft
ORIENTATION: Acidic

SPEYSIDE GLENLIVET

STILL

LIGHT

ESTABLISHED 1991

Good water makes good whisky, and the still version of this slightly alkaline, low TDS water is the perfect match for your single-malt whisky.

The spring, located in Speyside away from habitation, industry, and agriculture, is locally known as Slochd. Speyside produces more single-malt whisky than any other part of the world. Quartzite at the source keeps high levels of minerals from mixing with the water. The bottling plant was built in 1991, with a pipeline leading to the stainless steel springhead. The European Union recognized Speyside Glenlivet as a natural mineral water in 1998.

Ballindalloch,
UNITED KINGDOM

CARBONATION 5 mg/l artificial TDS 64 mg/l HARDNESS 41 mg/l pH 7.7 NITRATE <1 mg/l CALCIUM 13 mg/l MAGNESIUM 2 mg/l SODIUM 4 mg/l POTASSIUM 1 mg/l BICARBONATE 45 mg/l SULFATES 5 mg/l CHLORIDES 6 mg/l

VIRGINALITY: ♦ ♦ ♦ ♦ ♦

REGION: Banffshire, Scotland

SOURCE: Spring at 1,520 feet (463 m)

MINERALITY: Low

HARDNESS: Slightly Hard

ORIENTATION: Hint of Sweet

ST. GEORGES

STILL

St. Georges, currently only available as still water, is very light, surprisingly soft, and very close to neutral in pH. Of course, the main attraction is high-concept bottle.

A remote Corsican mountain 3,500 feet (1,067 m) above sea level is home to the St. Georges spring. The water's very low mineral content comes from local granite. The unspoiled source offers a great water, which the company presents in a very linear plastic bottle designed by Philippe Starck and inspired by medicine bottles from ancient Rome. The black bottle cap symbolizes Corsica's black flag.

Serra-Cimaggia,
FRANCE

TDS 140 mg/l **HARDNESS** 23 mg/l **PH** 6.8 **NITRATE** <1 mg/l
CALCIUM 5 mg/l **MAGNESIUM** 2 mg/l **SODIUM** 4 mg/l
POTASSIUM 1 mg/l **BICARBONATE** 30 mg/l **SULFATES** 6 mg/l
CHLORIDES 25 mg/l

VIRGINALITY: ♦ ♦ ♦ ♦ ♦

REGION: Corsica

SOURCE: Spring at 3,500 feet (1,067 m)

MINERAL CONTENT: Low

HARDNESS: Slightly Hard

TASTE: Neutral

STONECLEAR SPRINGS

STILL

ESTABLISHED 2005

The award-winning water of StoneClear Springs is sold under its own name, but the company also offers many custom glass and PET bottles for private-label bottling.

The spring 60 miles (97 km) west of Nashville is surrounded by 120 acres (49 hectares) of virgin forest; the same family has owned the spring for two centuries. Bottling at the source prevents the water from being exposed to air, which could introduce contaminants.

Vanleer, USA

TDS 140 mg/l **HARDNESS** 125 mg/l **pH** 7.3 **NITRATE** <1 mg/l
CALCIUM 50 mg/l **MAGNESIUM** 0 mg/l **SODIUM** 0 mg/l
POTASSIUM 0 mg/l **BICARBONATE** 140 mg/l **SULFATES** 0 mg/l
CHLORIDES 2 mg/l

VIRGINALITY: ◆ ◆ ◆ ◆ ◆
REGION: Tennessee
SOURCE: Spring
MINERALITY: Low
HARDNESS: Hard
ORIENTATION: Neutral

SUNLIGHT SPRINGS

STILL   BOLD

A medium mineral content water from a pristine and remote source, Sunlight Springs comes in a premium blue glass bottle with a crown cap. Unfortunately, the water is not as well-known as it should be and gets little distribution.

Mountainous terrain keeps the source protected from development. Before surfacing at the spring, rain and snow on a granite peak in the Rockies spend two to three thousand years filtering through sedimentary rock formed by the beds and shores of ancient oceans. Gravity feeds the water through stainless steel pipes to a bottling facility east of Yellowstone National Park.

Yellowstone
Headwaters Ranch,
USA

CARBONATION artificial **TDS** 288 mg/l **HARDNESS** 189 mg/l **pH** 7.8 **NITRATE** <1 mg/l **CALCIUM** 53 mg/l **MAGNESIUM** 14 mg/l **SODIUM** 10 mg/l **POTASSIUM** 2 mg/l **BICARBONATE** 188 mg/l **SULFATES** 116 mg/l **CHLORIDES** 1 mg/l

VIRGINALITY: ◆ ◆ ◆ ◆

REGION: Wyoming

SOURCE: Spring

MINERALITY: Medium

HARDNESS: Very Hard

ORIENTATION: Alkaline

VINTAGE: 4,000 years

TAU

STILL | LIGHT

This nice, low mineral content water comes with a high-concept, minimalist presentation (think W Hotels). The almost neutral pH sometimes triggers a sweet perception. Tau matches a great water with a great bottle—something that is not always the case.

Tau is an ancient Welsh word meaning "to be silent"—an appropriate name for the bottle's stark, monochrome design. The contemporary, understated package is aimed at designer restaurants, bars, cafés, and hotels, where elegance and purity are valued over flashy color.

Wales,
UNITED KINGDOM

CARBONATION artificial **TDS** 208 mg/l **HARDNESS** 126 mg/l **pH** 7.2 **NITRATE** <1 mg/l **CALCIUM** 31 mg/l **MAGNESIUM** 12 mg/l **SODIUM** 21mg/l **POTASSIUM** 1 mg/l **SILICA** 13.5 mg/l **BICARBONATE** 88 mg/l **SULFATES** 28 mg/l **CHLORIDES** 21 mg/l

VIRGINALITY: ♦ ♦ ♦ ♦ ♦
REGION: Wales
SOURCE: Well
MINERALITY: Low
HARDNESS: Very Hard
ORIENTATION: Neutral

TIPPERARY

ESTABLISHED 1986

STILL · BOLD

The interesting taste of Tipperary may come from the potassium level. The water's loud but not overpowering bubbles are perfect for mixed drinks, if you don't mind the sodium. The bicarbonate is beneficial for digestion, and the superior, low level of nitrate indicates a pristine source.

Since its founding in 1986, Tipperary Natural Mineral Water has become a highly visible Irish brand. The Devil's Bit Mountains in County Tipperary act as a filter; water at the source is especially filtered and protected by sandstone from the Devonian Period.

Devil's Bit Mountain,
IRELAND

CARBONATION artificial TDS 272 mg/l HARDNESS 185 mg/l pH 7.7 NITRATE <1 mg/l CALCIUM 37 mg/l MAGNESIUM 23 mg/l SODIUM 25 mg/l POTASSIUM 17 mg/l SILICA NA BICARBONATE 282 mg/l SULFATES 10 mg/l CHLORIDES 15 mg/l

VIRGINALITY: ♦ ♦ ♦ ♦ ♦
REGION: Borrisoleigh
SOURCE: Spring at 330 feet (100 m)
MINERALITY: Medium
HARDNESS: Hard
ORIENTATION: Hint of Sweet

TRINITY
(ORIGINAL)

STILL

Trinity Original is a soft, low mineral content water with a very alkaline pH and high levels of silica and sodium. It comes from a pristine source.

Geothermal pressure brings Trinity to the surface through granite faults with crystalline linings. The water emerges with a high temperature of 138 degrees Fahrenheit (59°C), and it is more than sixteen thousand years old.

Batholith Mountains,
USA

TDS 195 mg/l **HARDNESS** 6 mg/l **pH** 9.6 **NITRATE** <1 mg/l
CALCIUM 1.4 mg/l **MAGNESIUM** <1 mg/l **SODIUM** 49 mg/l
POTASSIUM 1 mg/l **SILICA** 75 mg/l **BICARBONATE** 48 mg/l
SULFATES 18 mg/l **CHLORIDES** 3 mg/l

VIRGINALITY: ◆ ◆ ◆ ◆ ◆
REGION: Idaho
SOURCE: Spring at 4,500 feet (1,372 m)
MINERALITY: Low
HARDNESS: Soft
ORIENTATION: Alkaline
VINTAGE: 16,000 years

TY NANT

Established 1976

STILL   CLASSIC

The bubbles in the artificially carbonated version of Ty Nant (pronounced "Tee Nant," which rhymes with ant) are fairly loud and should be paired with food that has a substantial mouthfeel so the water is not overpowered. I love still Ty Nant's low mineral content, almost neutral pH, and very pristine source. The great water is packaged in an equally great blue glass bottle—probably the most recognizable one on the market.

Ty Nant's aquifer is made up of metamorphic mudstone, siltstone, and sandstone dating from the Silurian period. Organic management (for the past decade) of the land near the source and daily chemical monitoring ensure the quality of the water; the very low nitrate level reflects the care the company takes in protecting its product.

Bethania,
United Kingdom

CARBONATION artificial **TDS** 165 mg/l **HARDNESS** 103 mg/l **pH** 6.8 **NITRATE** <1 mg/l **CALCIUM** 22 mg/l **MAGNESIUM** 12 mg/l **SODIUM** 22 mg/l **POTASSIUM** 1 mg/l **BICARBONATE** 116 mg/l **SULFATES** 4 mg/l **CHLORIDES** 14 mg/l

VIRGINALITY: ♦ ♦ ♦ ♦

REGION: Wales

SOURCE: Spring at 689 feet (210 m)

MINERALITY: Low

HARDNESS: Moderately Hard

ORIENTATION: Neutral

VELLAMO

Established 1993

STILL

EFFERVESCENT

Vellamo, packaged in an upscale glass bottle, is very old water with a medium TDS and a neutral pH. The water was formed before industrial pollution even existed.

Ice Age rainwater filled a gap between rock layers in a ravine beneath Rääveli Lake; the gap was then gradually sealed with a layer of impervious rock. In the thousands of years the water spent in this aquifer, it absorbed minerals from the rock but was undisturbed by modern pollution. Carbon dating places the age of the water at five to eight thousand years, though fifteen to thirty percent of the water may be ten thousand years old or older.

Viikinäinen,
Finland

CARBONATION 2mg/l artificial **TDS** 518 mg/l **HARDNESS** 228 mg/l **pH** 7.1 **NITRATE** <1 mg/l **CALCIUM** 59 mg/l **MAGNESIUM** 20 mg/l **SODIUM** 120 mg/l **POTASSIUM** 4mg/l **SILICA** 14mg/l **BICARBONATE** 160 mg/l **SULFATES** 47 mg/l **CHLORIDES** 220 mg/l

VIRGINALITY: ◆ ◆ ◆ ◆ ◆

REGION: Heinola

SOURCE: Well

MINERALITY: Medium

HARDNESS: Hard

ORIENTATION: Neutral

VINTAGE: 8,000 years

VIA NATURAL

STILL

This award-winning, very low mineral content water comes in a stunning PET bottle, which fits well in an epicurean setting.

Sandovalina is about 375 miles (600 km) from the Brazilian capital in the state of São Paulo. No industry is present near the falls and cataracts surrounding the remote Fonte Sant'Ana spring, from which water emerges at 75 degrees Fahrenheit (24°C) and is piped to the bottling plant.

Sandovalina,
BRAZIL

TDS 85 mg/l **HARDNESS** 21 mg/l **pH** 6.1 **NITRATE** 7.6 mg/l
CALCIUM 5 mg/l **MAGNESIUM** 2 mg/l **SODIUM** 4 mg/l
POTASSIUM 2 mg/l **BICARBONATE** 28 mg/l **SULFATES** <1 mg/l
CHLORIDES 2 mg/l

VIRGINALITY: ♦ ♦

REGION: São Paulo

SOURCE: Spring

MINERALITY: Low

HARDNESS: Slightly Hard

ORIENTATION: Acidic

VICHY CATALAN

ESTABLISHED 1889

CLASSIC

The best-known mineral water from Spain, Vichy Catalan has very high mineral content, natural carbonation, and an almost neutral pH.

Archaeological evidence suggests the area near Caldes de Malavella has had a human population since prehistoric times. The many local sources of effervescent, thermal water were likely a major attraction. Both springs draw from a single aquifer, though each water emerges with slightly different compositions. Vichy Catalan water was first bottled in 1889, and an influx of visitors led to the construction of a spa soon after. Water and carbon dioxide gas are harvested separately from the source, which is capped to control the output; after the water has cooled from 140 degrees Fahrenheit (60°C), the gas is added back in.

Caldes de Malavella, SPAIN

CARBONATION natural TDS 2,900 mg/l HARDNESS 61 mg/l pH 8 NITRATE <1 mg/l CALCIUM 14 mg/l MAGNESIUM 6 mg/l SODIUM 1,100 mg/l POTASSIUM 44 mg/l SILICA 77 mg/l BICARBONATE 2,081 mg/l SULFATES 46 mg/l CHLORIDES 680 mg/l

VIRGINALITY: ◆ ◆ ◆ ◆ ◆

REGION: Girona, Catalonia

SOURCE: Spring

MINERALITY: Very High

HARDNESS: Hard

ORIENTATION: Alkaline

VITTEL

Established 1854

STILL

Vittel comes from a pristine source and is a still, medium minerality water with a hint of sweetness due to a pH of 7.3. A high level of bicarbonate makes this water beneficial for the digestive system.

About three feet (1 m) of rain falls each year in western Vosges. Some rain seeps into the water table, so the source is constantly refreshed. The village of Vittel is popular with the Club Med crowd. The ancients knew the three springs: Bonne Source, which is bottled; Grande Source, which imparts high levels of calcium, bicarbonate, and sulfates; and Hépar, with water very high in calcium and sulfates.

Vittel,
France

TDS 403 mg/l HARDNESS 308 mg/l pH 7.3 NITRATE
0.6 mg/l CALCIUM 91 mg/l MAGNESIUM 20 mg/l SODIUM
7 mg/l POTASSIUM 5 mg/l SILICA 9 mg/l BICARBONATE
258 mg/l SULFATES 105 mg/l CHLORIDES 4 mg/l

VIRGINALITY: ♦ ♦ ♦ ♦ ♦

REGION: Vosges

SOURCE: Spring at 1,115 feet (340 m)

MINERALITY: Medium

HARDNESS: Very Hard

ORIENTATION: Neutral

VODA VODA

ESTABLISHED 2004

STILL

The source of Voda Voda has long been associated with healing. The medium mineral content water has a nice level of bicarbonate and comes in a very modern plastic bottle that looks great on the table.

Vrujci Spa, at the foot of the Toplica River valley's Suvobor Mountains, first gained fame in the late nineteenth century. Bottled at the 896-foot-deep (273 m) source, the water is filtered by limestone and not treated with chemicals.

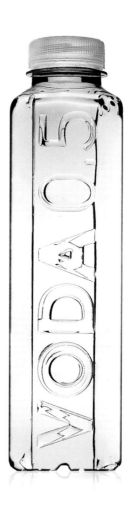

Vrujci Spa,
SERBIA

TDS 383 mg/l HARDNESS 259 mg/l pH 7.23 NITRATE 1.8 mg/l CALCIUM 78 mg/l MAGNESIUM 16 mg/l SODIUM 38 mg/l POTASSIUM 3 mg/l BICARBONATE 390 mg/l SULFATES 16 mg/l CHLORIDES 9 mg/l

VIRGINALITY: ♦ ♦ ♦ ♦

REGION: Kolubara

SOURCE: Spring

MINERALITY: Medium

HARDNESS: Very Hard

ORIENTATION: Neutral

VOLVIC

ESTABLISHED 1938

STILL

Volvic, as the name implies, has a volcanic origin, which is most evident in the water's level of silica. The water has a very neutral but slightly soft taste.

Volvic mineral water originates as rain at a high elevation in central France's Auvergne National Park. Volcanic rock and sand slowly filter the water and give it a low level of minerals on its way to the massive aquifer. The water surfaces at 46 degrees Fahrenheit (8°C) and is bottled before it can be exposed to the environment.

Clairvic Spring,
FRANCE

TDS 130 mg/l **HARDNESS** 62 mg/l **pH** 7 **NITRATE** 1.4 mg/l
CALCIUM 12 mg/l **MAGNESIUM** 8mg/l **SODIUM** 12 mg/l
POTASSIUM 6 mg/l **SILICA** 32 mg/l **BICARBONATE** 71 mg/l
SULFATES 8 mg/l **CHLORIDES** 14 mg/l

VIRGINALITY: ♦ ♦ ♦ ♦
REGION: Auvergne
SOURCE: Spring
MINERALITY: Low
HARDNESS: Slightly Hard
ORIENTATION: Neutral

VÖSLAUER

STILL   LIGHT

Established 1936

A very prominent brand in Austria, Vöslauer is available in Still and in two sparkling versions, both of which by the numbers have to be designated Light. But they straddle the Effervescent (the mild version) and Classic (the prickelned version) designations. The water is often used for spritzer.

Bad Vöslau's spa is ancient, though Vöslauer water wasn't bottled for commercial purposes until 1936. The water is about ten thousand years old and rises by artesian pressure from a depth of more than 1,800 feet (550 m); the water remains unpolluted while beneath the surface.

Bad Vöslau,
Austria

CARBONATION 3 mg/l, 5 mg/l artificial TDS 691 mg/l HARDNESS 447 mg/l pH 7.6 NITRATE 2 mg/l CALCIUM 110 mg/l MAGNESIUM 43 mg/l SODIUM 11 mg/l POTASSIUM 2 mg/l SILICA 13 mg/l BICARBONATE 255 mg/l SULFATES 229 mg/l CHLORIDES 21 mg/l

VIRGINALITY: ♦ ♦ ♦ ♦
REGION: Niederösterreich
SOURCE: Artesian
MINERALITY: Medium
HARDNESS: Very Hard
ORIENTATION: Hint of Sweet
VINTAGE: 10,000 years

VOSS

Established 1998

STILL · EFFERVESCENT

Voss's most recognizable feature is its highly designed—some say over-designed—bottle. There is a distinct difference between Voss Still and Voss Sparkling: The sparkling version is augmented with bicarbonate to bring its TDS to 295 mg/l (as opposed to just 22 mg/l for the still version). I don't think Voss needs to polish its sparkling water in this way, which forces an otherwise natural product into the processed water category.

Though the name might lead you to think the water comes from mountains near Voss, western Norway, it in fact comes from that country's south coast—specifically, the remote, thinly populated Iveland area, northeast of Kristiansand. Rock and ice have protected the artesian source for hundreds of years.

Iveland,
NORWAY

CARBONATION artificial TDS 22 mg/l (still), 295 mg/l (sparkling) HARDNESS 14 mg/l pH 6.5 NITRATE <1 mg/l CALCIUM 4 mg/l MAGNESIUM 1 mg/l SODIUM 4 mg/l POTASSIUM NA SILICA NA BICARBONATE NA SULFATES NA CHLORIDES NA

VIRGINALITY: ♦ ♦ ♦ ♦ ♦

REGION: Southern Coast

SOURCE: Artesian

MINERALITY: Super Low (still),
　　Medium (sparkling)

HARDNESS: Soft

ORIENTATION: Acidic

WAIWERA INFINITY

<small>ESTABLISHED 1870</small>

STILL

This enhanced water comes from a source with a long history. The current bottle is a modern interpretation of the traditional glass bottle, which dates from the nineteenth century.

Visitors to the Waiwera Resort began taking this water, which is naturally heated, in the 1870s. Today, the water is treated by carbon filtration, heat exchange, cooling, ultraviolet sterilization, softening, and reverse osmosis after traveling up a 1,300-foot (400 m) borehole. In a stainless steel tank, the company adds a special blend of calcium, potassium, magnesium, sodium, and mineral salts.

Waiwera Resort,
NEW ZEALAND

TDS 120 mg/l HARDNESS 40 mg/l pH 9 NITRATE <1 mg/l
CALCIUM 12 mg/l MAGNESIUM 3 mg/l SODIUM 2 mg/l
POTASSIUM 3 mg/l BICARBONATE 20 mg/l SULFATES 1 mg/l
CHLORIDES 30 mg/l

VIRGINALITY: ♦ ♦ ♦ ♦ ♦
REGION: North Island
SOURCE: Artesian
MINERALITY: Low
HARDNESS: Slightly Hard
ORIENTATION: Alkaline

WATTWILLER

Established 1924

STILL EFFERVESCENT

This great water also has a great story—it's very rare to find sources of both still and naturally carbonated water so close to each other. The presentation is also admirable, with both plastic and glass options available.

The source was discovered by the Romans, and the Abbey of Murbach watched over the spring from 735 BCE. The German name for the village where the source is found, Wasserweiler, means "village of water." A large swath of protected woodland surrounds the aquifer, which is 30 feet (9 m) below the surface. Still mineral water emerges from the Lithinee spring with a slightly different composition than the naturally carbonated water from the Jouvence spring.

Village de Wattwiller,
FRANCE

LITHINEE: **TDS** 889 mg/l **HARDNESS** 627 mg/l **pH** 7.6 **NITRATE** <1 mg/l **CALCIUM** 222 mg/l **MAGNESIUM** 18 mg/l **SODIUM** 4 mg/l **POTASSIUM** 2 mg/l **BICARBONATE** 142 mg/l **SULFATES** 520 mg/l **CHLORIDES** 5 mg/l

JOUVENCE: **CARBONATION** natural **TDS** 501 mg/l **HARDNESS** 379 mg/l **pH** 5 **NITRATE** <1 mg/l **CALCIUM** 126 mg/l **MAGNESIUM** 16 mg/l **SODIUM** 3 mg/l **POTASSIUM** 2 mg/l **BICARBONATE** 167 mg/l **SULFATES** 223 mg/l **CHLORIDES** 6 mg/l

VIRGINALITY: ◆ ◆ ◆ ◆ ◆

REGION: Alsace

SOURCE: Spring

MINERALITY: High (still), Medium (sparkling)

HARDNESS: Very Hard

ORIENTATION: Hint of Sweet (still), Acidic (sparkling)

WHISTLER

STILL

LIGHT

ESTABLISHED 1993

The glass bottle contains water from a pristine source with super low TDS and a neutral pH. Available Still and artificially carbonated to a Light level, Whistler is perfect for mixed drinks.

Spetch Creek lies in British Columbia's Coastal Mountains, which run down the coast of the province about 62 miles (100 km) from the Pacific coast. The mountains are a popular skiing destination. Loose glacial deposits on a layer of gray-white granite filter groundwater that comes in off the ocean as rain and snow before flowing to the aquifer about 65 feet (20 m) below the surface of the Spetch Creek alluvial fan. Pressure in the aquifer brings the water up to a depth of 30 feet (9 m).

Spetch Creek,
Pemberton, CANADA

CARBONATION 3.2 mg/l artificial TDS 48 mg/l HARDNESS 21 mg/l pH 7 NITRATE <1 mg/l CALCIUM 12 mg/l MAGNESIUM 1 mg/l SODIUM 2 mg/l BICARBONATE 20 mg/l SULFATES 8 mg/l CHLORIDES 3 mg/l

VIRGINALITY: ♦ ♦ ♦ ♦ ♦

REGION: British Columbia

SOURCE: Well

MINERALITY: Super Low

HARDNESS: Slightly Hard

ORIENTATION: Neutral

WILDALP

ESTABLISHED 2002

STILL

In addition to the regular version, Wildalp also offers water that has been bottled during a full moon, lending it the German description Vollmondabfüllung. *Its bottle is similar to the standard package but with a different label, and the water is alleged to have added health and wellness benefits.*

Wildalp water comes from Styria's Hochschwab region, near the source of Vienna's esteemed municipal drinking water, Wiener Hochquellwasser ("Viennese high-altitude spring water"), which is carried to the city by an aqueduct. Wildalp, filtered by Alpine limestone, has little sodium but a high 9.2 mg/l of oxygen.

Wildalp,
AUSTRIA

TDS 178 mg/l HARDNESS 160 mg/l pH 7.8 NITRATE 3.7 mg/l CALCIUM 45 mg/l MAGNESIUM 12 mg/l SODIUM 2 mg/l BICARBONATE 196 mg/l SULFATES 12 mg/l CHLORIDES 3 mg/l

VIRGINALITY: ◆ ◆ ◆ ◆
REGION: Styria
SOURCE: Spring
MINERALITY: Low
HARDNESS: Hard
ORIENTATION: Alkaline

PART III

WATERS BY COUNTRY

BOTTLING COUNTRIES

ARGENTINA

- About 25 brands

Growth is predicted in Argentina's consumption of bottled water, as in the rest of the world. Exciting waters from uninhabited parts of the country are entering the American and European markets—Argentina's water may soon have a reputation to match that of its high-quality beef.

| Lauquen | Still, Classic | page 117 |

AUSTRALIA

- 4.5 gallons (17 l) per capita
- About 50 brands

Low per capita consumption of bottled water leaves much room for the industry to grow. Experts in the Australian water industry say four sources along the Great Dividing Range mountains—the Gold Coast hinterland, Peat's Ridge, the Southern Highlands, and the

Ballarat district—supply almost ninety percent of the country's bottled water (including water that is processed before bottling). More minor sources in the same mountain range, including those in Dorrigo, Lithgow, and the Snowy Mountains, account for another eight percent; springs in Tasmania and southern and western Australia provide the remaining two percent. I think the remote, unspoiled environment of Tasmania produces some of Australia's most exciting waters.

Cape Grim	Still, Effervescent	page	79
Cloud Juice	Still	page	83
Diamond	Still	page	87

AUSTRIA

- 23 gallons (87 l) per capita
- About 50 brands

Healing waters (*Heilwasser* in German) and spas were the center of Austria's bottled water industry during the eighteenth and nineteenth centuries, as was the case throughout Europe. Many waters used in that period have very high mineral content; they were often sourced from hot volcanic or geothermal springs.

Austrians care about the water they drink and tend not to drink it on the go. For a population of about eight million, the country has a highly developed bottled water industry selling about fifty brands of water. Vöslauer, Römerquelle, and other major brands dominate sales, but smaller, local water brands should not be overlooked. Still waters are often accompanied by a mildly carbonated version and a sparkling *prickelned* water.

Römerquelle	Still, Light, Classic	page 139
Vöslauer	Still, Light	page 165

Wildalp	Still	page 170

BELGIUM

- 31 gallons (117 l) per capita
- About 50 brands

Belgium became an independent nation in 1831 and now houses the European Union's headquarters. Discovered in Roman times, the mineral waters of the town of Spa in the Ardennes remain well-known. The country's bottled water comes from an estimated fifteen springs and thirty-five thermal water sources.

Chaudfontaine	Still, Bold	page 82
Spa	Still, Light	page 150

BRAZIL

- About 80 brands

The Brazilian mineral water industry is very well regulated and organized—perhaps the best outside Europe. Three hundred mineral water springs and one hundred spas give Brazilians much to choose from, and the large country's geological diversity produces waters with a range of mineral content. Most of these waters have a wide distribution within the country.

Via Natural	Still	page 160

BULGARIA

- About 15 brands

We will see more bottled water coming from Bulgaria, which currently has a relatively underdeveloped market, after the country's expected European Union accession in 2007.

| Pelagonia | Still, Light | page 134 |

CANADA

- 8 gallons (30 l) per capita
- About 70 brands

Canada is ripe with unspoiled land and pristine water sources. People in Québec appreciate bottled mineral water in a way similar to the French; many English and French Canadians are regular drinkers of bottled water. The last decade has seen rapid growth of the industry. The Canadian government regulates bottled water as a food under the Food and Drugs Act.

Canaqua	Still	page 78
Ice Age	Still	page 110
I Litre	Still	page 131
Saint-Élie	Still	page 140
Saint-Justin	Still, Bold	page 141
Whistler	Still, Light	page 169

FIJI

- 2 brands

This South Pacific island is famed for its eponymous water brand. Fiji Water took Aqua Fiji to court to protect that brand name, and the latter company must now do business as Aqua Pacific.

| Aqua Pacific | Still | page 73 |
| Fiji | Still | page 96 |

FINLAND

- About 15 brands

Finland has the world's best water according to a UN report published at the Third World Water Forum, beating out Canada, New
Zealand, Great Britain, and Japan (in that order). This recognized
quality makes it surprising that the most popular Finnish water,
Vichy Original, is manufactured with a specific composition rather
than bottled from a natural source. Its mineral composition is similar to the French Vichy Célestins, which was likely used as a model.

Vellamo	Still, Effervescent	page 159

FRANCE

- 38 gallons (145 l) per capita
- About 200 brands

The French tradition of therapeutic use of mineral water dates back
to the Roman period, when spas were built at the sources of Badoit,
Perrier, and Vittel. Brands like Perrier and Evian enjoy a global reputation as luxury waters. The French drink nearly as much bottled
water per capita was as the top-drinking Italians. The French care
about their water and often drink it in an epicurean setting. Almost
1,200 sources of mineral water are estimated to exist in France; most
are used medically in spas, and only a small number of the sources
provide water for bottling.

Badoit	Effervescent	page 74
Celtic	Still, Light, Classic	page 80
Chateldon	Light	page 81
Contrex	Still	page 84
Cristaline (St. Cecile)	Still	page 85
Evian	Still	page 93

Perrier	Bold	page 135
St. Georges	Still	page 152
Vittel	Still	page 162
Volvic	Still	page 164
Wattwiller	Still, Effervescent	page 168

GERMANY

- 29 gallons (109 l) per capita
- About 450 brands

Sources of German mineral water, of which there are about 230, have been known since Roman times. Health resorts and spas testify to the long-standing German notion of *Heilwasser*, or "healing waters." Sparkling and often highly carbonated water is preferred by Germans; as such, most German waters are carbonated.

Apollinaris	Still, Classic	page 72
Gerolsteiner	Still, Light, Classic	page 101
Selters	Still, Light, Bold	page 148

ICELAND

- About 10 brands

Iceland's sparse population—not quite 5 people per square mile (3 per sq km)—is confined mostly to the coasts of the 40,000-square-mile (103,000 sq km) island. The less inhabited interior of the country is thus a good place to source water; the unspoiled reputation of the country is also a marketing advantage.

| Icelandic Glacial | Still | page 111 |
| Iceland Spring | Still | page 112 |

IRELAND

- 7 gallons (27 l) per capita
- About 12 brands

Increases in disposable income and health-consciousness in Ireland have encouraged growth in the country's bottled water industry, which continues to expand rapidly.

Eauzone	Still, Light, Classic	page	90
Tipperary	Still, Bold	page	156

ITALY

- 50 gallons (189 l) per capita
- About 600 brands

Italy is the epicenter of water connoisseurship. With more than six hundred native brands to choose from, Italians lead the world in per capita consumption. Though Americans drink thirty-five percent of their water on the go, the Italian figure is only six percent—these serious water drinkers apparently sit down to savor their water. Locals often prefer regional waters with limited distribution that are not exported.

Bernina	Still	page	75
Daggio	Still, Effervescent	page	86
Ducale	Still, Effervescent	page	89
Ferrarelle	Effervescent	page	95
Fiuggi	Still, Bold	page	98
Galvanina	Still, Classic	page	100
Goccia di Carnia	Still, Effervescent	page	103
Kaiser Wasser	Still, Bold	page	113
Lauretana	Still, Bold	page	118
Levissima	Still, Effervescent	page	120

JAPAN

- 3.5 gallons (10 l) per capita
- About 450 brands

The disparity between Japan's low consumption of bottled water and the country's high number of brands means there's much room for growth in the Japanese market. Local bottled waters are preferred at home; hotels, restaurants, and bars serve well-known imported brands. Only a handful of Japanese waters, such as Finé, are exported and known outside Japan.

NEW ZEALAND

- 1.5 gallons (5 l) per capita
- About 20 brands

New Zealand is just realizing that its remote, unspoiled sources have great potential to serve the bottled water trend. Those sources often supply low TDS water.

Waiwera Infinity	Still	page 167

NORWAY

- 5.5 gallons (21 l) per capita
- About 10 brands

The trendy, high-concept Voss is Norway's main international offering.

Voss	Still, Effervescent	page 166

ROMANIA

- About 20 brands

The geological diversity of Romania produces a wide range of mineral waters, though these waters are not well-known in the United States. The Romans, however, did know the Romanian springs, which produce water historically popular in Europe. The popularity was especially notable during the Austro-Hungarian Empire—Borsec was a favorite of Emperor Franz Joseph.

Borsec	Light	page 77
Harghita	Effervescent	page 105

SERBIA

- About 20 brands

Mineral and curative sparkling waters have long been bottled in Serbia, which is abundant in water sources. The industry has largely bounced back from the economic hardship of the late nineties, and still water is a rapidly growing sector despite the sparkling tradition.

Voda Voda	Still	page 163

SLOVENIA

- About 15 brands

Great mineral water has a long tradition in this former Yugoslav republic and new EU member state. Radenska, from near the border with Austria, is especially well-known.

Donat Mg	Light	page 88
Radenska	Light	page 137

SOUTH AFRICA

- About 40 brands

The popularity and quality of wine from South Africa have increased dramatically of late, with the country's bottled water industry riding the coattails. As a result, consumers have been interested in the local terroir of South African waters.

Karoo	Still, Light	page 114
L'Aubade	Still, Effervescent	page 116

SPAIN

- 32 gallons (120 l) per capita
- About 170 brands

The Spanish are the world's fourth-highest consumers of bottled water per capita; many observers predict they will pass the Italians and the French in the next five years. This high domestic consumption is at odds with Spanish waters' small international reputation. And though Spain has sources of naturally carbonated mineral water, still water is preferred by ninety-five percent of Spaniards.

Font Selva	Still	page 99

Malavella	Still, Classic	page 124
Mondariz	Still	page 127
Vichy Catalan	Classic	page 161

SWEDEN

- 5 gallons (19 l) per capita
- About 12 brands

Ramlösa virtually defines mineral water in Sweden. More than ninety percent of the market belongs to the brand, which also carries the label "By Special Warrant Purveyor to His Majesty the King of Sweden."

| Malmberg | Still, Light | page 125 |
| Ramlösa | Still, Light | page 138 |

UNITED KINGDOM

- 6.5 gallons (25 l) per capita
- About 150 brands

Water from sources all over the UK is bottled and distributed locally, but some British waters are internationally distributed. Ty Nant and a few others are among the most globally recognizable brands.

Gleneagles	Still, Light	page 102
Hadham	Still, Classic	page 104
Harrogate Spa	Still, Classic	page 106
Highland Spring	Still, Light	page 108
Hildon	Still, Light	page 109
Llanllyr Source	Still, Effervescent	page 121
Speyside Glenlivet	Still, Light	page 151
Tau	Still, Light	page 155
Ty Nant	Still, Classic	page 158

UNITED STATES

- 18 gallons (69 l) per capita
- About 180 brands

Perrier spent $6 million on the 1977 advertising campaign that started the U.S. bottled water trend, and interest in natural foods and the spread of health food stores further encouraged bottled water consumption. Bottled water carries connotations of health, fitness, and sports in the United States but is not often found in an epicurean setting. This is unsurprising given that purified municipal tap water accounts for forty percent of bottled water sold and consumed in the United States.

Bling H$_2$O	Still	page	76
Eldorado	Still	page	91
English Mountain	Still	page	92
Famous Crazy Water	Still	page	94
Hawaiian Springs	Still	page	107
Kona Deep	Still	page	115
Le Bleu	Still	page	119
Manitou	Still	page	126
Montaqua	Still	page	128
Mountain Valley Spring	Still, Classic	page	129
Mount Olympus	Still	page	130
Oregon Rain	Still	page	132
Saratoga	Still, Bold	page	146
Seawright Springs	Still	page	147
StoneClear Springs	Still	page	153
Sunlight Springs	Still, Bold	page	154
Trinity (Original)	Still	page	157

INDEX

ACKNOWLEDGMENTS

The author would like to acknowledge the help of many individuals, institutions, and companies in compiling the information necessary to write this book. Special thanks go to Chris Middleton of FountainHeadPeople.com; the History of Bottled Water section in this book is based on a series of articles he wrote for the FineWaters Web site. Thanks also to Lars Dahmann, Steve Rowe, and Margaret Magnus. The book would be much poorer without the help of Gene D. Donney of AquaMaestro.com, who shared his deep knowledge and passion for the bottled water industry with us. Thanks to Dr. Chaikin, my cardiologist, without whom I probably would not have written the book. A special thanks to my wife, Erika, and our families for their support.

ABOUT THE AUTHOR

Michael Mascha is the founder and publisher of FineWaters (www.finewaters.com), a Web site portal that is the definitive voice for water connoisseurs and their lifestyle. The site, with its thriving online community, is the leading destination for consumer education and resources in the $9-billion bottled water industry.

Mascha holds a PhD in Anthropology and Communication Science from the University of Vienna and lives with his wife and their Australian cattle dog in Los Angeles.